D1712087

The
Violent
Game

The Violent Game

by Gary Ronberg

A Rutledge Book
Prentice-Hall, Inc.
Englewood Cliffs, N.J.

Library of Congress Cataloging in Publication Data
Ronberg, Gary.
  The violent game.
  A Rutledge book.
  1. Hockey. I. Title.
GV847.R623   796.9'62   75-20238
ISBN 0-13-942136-X

Contents

The Game within the Game

The word "violence" has been so often applied to hockey that I want to make clear at the outset how I intend to deal with it in this book. Violence is not necessarily against the rules; some perfectly legal tactics can be quite violent—a body check, for example. On the other hand, breaking the rules is not always violent. Some fouls are almost gentle—a hold or a trip, for example. So I prefer the term "violent fouling," rather than just "violence" or "aggressiveness," for that part of the game that is both violent and against the rules.

I realize that "violent fouling" is an imprecise term, but I have taken it to mean breaking the rules in a way likely to provoke a belligerent reaction. An elbow to the face is a violent foul; a hook to stop a breakaway is not.

Violent fouling is not always dangerous. Whereas stick swinging is violent fouling that jeopardizes players' careers, even their lives, fighting is violent fouling that usually hurts no one seriously.

Nor is violent fouling always bad. It can ruin a good game, but it can spice up a dull one, even transform it into a good game.

Violent fouling *is* important. It is as much a part of pro hockey as scoring and goaltending, and more a part of hockey than of any other major sport. This book is an attempt to understand this aspect of hockey, this game within a game. I feel sure that, in many respects, the game of violent fouling holds the key to understanding hockey as a whole—the most fascinating and wonderful spectator sport I know.

Finally, a word about the proposals I have made at the end of this book. I have criticized pro hockey under the assumption that the game would not be worth criticizing if it were not basically a good one. I realize that in some of my views I disagree with the people who run the game, but I trust these are honest differences of opinion among people who share an affection for the game and a desire to see it prosper.

Gary Ronberg
Chesterfield, Missouri
June, 1975

Introduction: The Tradition of Violence

Hockey has always been a violent game. It may even owe its name to violence. According to legend, the game, as it was first observed by European settlers in North America, was played by Iroquois Indians who cried "Ho-gee!" ("It hurts!") when they were slashed by errant swipes of the stick. This theory of derivation may be fanciful, but there was nothing fanciful about the game itself as the Indians played it. With hundreds of braves on each side, and few restrictions on what they could do to one another, hockey was more a war than a game. Serious injuries, even fatalities, were common.

In supposedly more civilized societies too, hockey was uncivilized. In 1862, a London newspaper, perhaps the first to condemn violence on ice, proclaimed, "Hockey . . . ought to be sternly forbidden, as it is not only annoying [to skaters at leisure on a pond] but dangerous. When a mass of human beings precipitates itself recklessly in any direction, accidents are certain to follow. . . . The game is by no means what it ought to be, as it is impossible to enforce the rules in such a miscellaneous assembly. . . . We should be truly glad to see the police interfere whenever hockey is commenced."

This was the game that found a home in Canada—wildly disorganized, confusing, and rough. With as many as thirty players on a side, hacking and colliding among themselves and their opponents, injuries were inevitable. And the mayhem endangered more than the participants. Warding off the cold by consuming great quantities of liquor, the spectators ringing the playing surface were not always nimble enough to escape when the play descended on them.

The goal judge stood behind the goalposts, dodging the puck and the players and making certain that his calls pleased the spirited audience—which was otherwise likely to lynch him. The referee was a moving target, but no less a homer. The home side could change him at will, and on one occasion a home team exercised its option eight times before it and its fans were satisfied.

Inevitably, this violent game produced horrible brutality. In 1907, a game between Ottawa and Montreal included several stick-swinging battles that moved the Montreal *Star* to call the game "an exhibition of butchery." Later that year Owen McCourt of Cornwall died the day after being struck in the head by a stick allegedly wielded by Montreal's Charles Masson. Masson was charged with murder, but acquitted when the judge was unable to determine whether it was Masson's stick or that of another opponent that killed McCourt.

A decade later, Bad Joe Hall of Montreal and Toronto's Alf Skinner were arrested and charged with disorderly conduct after a bitter stick-swinging duel in Toronto. They received suspended sentences.

The casualty toll gave hockey one of its fondest traditions—the players' resistance to injury. For decades the game's greatest response to its brutality has been in breeding players who can take it. After a game against the Montreal Wanderers, Jack Adams of the Toronto Arenas emerged so bloody that even his sister, a nurse at the hospital to which he was taken, was unable to recognize him when he was admitted. "When you got cut in those days," recalled Adams many years later, "you skated to the boards and the trainer sloshed off the blood with a sponge he kept in a bucket. Then he patched you up with a slice of adhesive tape. That night, most of my tape must have sweated off."

The early bad guys make the modern marauders seem mild-mannered. *Below:* Sprague Cleghorn; *below left:* Eddie Shore.

Despite some early attempts at disciplining violent offenders in the pro game, the bad guys flourished and injuries proliferated. In 1918–19, Seattle's Cully Wilson was thrown out of the Pacific Coast Hockey League for breaking the jaw of Vancouver's Mickey Mackay with a cross-check, only to join the National Hockey League the next year and become its penalty leader. In 1921–22, the infamous Sprague Cleghorn earned a match penalty (not only expulsion from the game but no substitute for 20 minutes) when he cut two Ottawa players and charged a third, sidelining all three for two games.

Eddie Shore, an All-Star defenseman for the Boston Bruins in the twenties and thirties, was one of the first players to win a sizable following in the United States. A performer of unquestioned skill, Shore was also one of the game's more vicious marauders. He was showered with fines, suspensions, and editorial condemnation, most of it richly deserved.

On December 12, 1933, he almost killed a man. During the second period of a game against the Toronto Maple Leafs at Boston Garden, Shore swept behind his net and started to carry the puck up ice. Suddenly, he was sent sprawling by one of the Maple Leafs. Furious over the check, Shore immediately took revenge on Toronto's Ace Bailey, whom he spotted heading back to the Leafs' zone. Shore leveled the Toronto player from behind, and Bailey fell backward, his skull striking the ice.

He lay unconscious for twenty minutes. Rushed to a nearby hospital, he underwent two brain operations the next day. A week later it was discovered that he had suffered two brain concussions, not one, and a third operation was performed. Bailey recovered, but never played hockey again.

The referees, the men who ostensibly controlled the violence, were more spectators than arbitrators. As early as 1926–27, NHL President Frank Calder suggested that it might take two referees to police the game, and his proposal was instituted briefly but with no significant effect. By the forties, the league had returned to one referee, who, in the words of former ref Bill Chadwick, "dropped the puck and folded his arms."

The violence of the game continued to victimize stars and scrubs alike. On March 28, 1950, the magnificent career of Detroit's Gordie Howe was nearly aborted in the first game of the Stanley Cup semifinals. Toronto's captain, Ted ("Teeder") Kennedy, was skating up the left

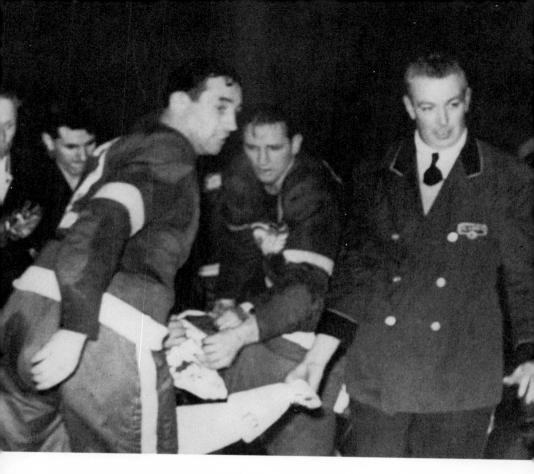

wing, pursued by Detroit's Black Jack Stewart, when Howe swept over from the right. Suddenly, the Red Wings' budding star was sent sprawling headfirst into the boards. Twice he tried to rise, only to fall back to the ice.

Howe was rushed to the hospital, where it was determined he had suffered a brain concussion, a slashed eyeball, and a nose fracture that extended under the injured eye. Worst of all, the doctors found severe hemorrhaging in the brain. Howe lay on the operating table for ninety minutes as a specialist sought to relieve the pressure between the brain and the skull. "When they opened up Gordie's skull," recalls Sid Abel, a teammate of Howe's at the time, "blood shot to the ceiling like a geyser."

Jack Evans and Larry Zeidel were two small-time victims. In 1952, during a game in the Western Hockey League, the two notorious bad men confronted each other

The violent game almost killed one of its brightest stars, Gordie Howe. Teammates Black Jack Stewart, left, and Sid Abel, rear, help carry the stretcher after Howe fractured his skull in 1950 playoffs.

in a horrifying stick-swinging duel. After breaking their sticks over each other's heads, they continued to flail away until their stick handles were reduced to nubs, their heads to masses of torn flesh, blood, and splinters.

Rowdiness among spectators, which had, like the other aspects of hockey violence, plagued the game from its beginning, erupted in a full-scale riot in 1955.

In March of that year, Maurice ("Rocket") Richard of the Canadiens was nearing the first scoring championship of his career when he carved up the face of Boston's Hal Laycoe. When linesman Cliff Thompson tried to intervene, Richard belted him in the eye. NHL President Clarence Campbell promptly suspended Richard for the

remainder of the season and the playoffs, costing the Montreal star his scoring championship and, quite possibly, the Canadiens the Stanley Cup.

Enraged people throughout Quebec flooded Campbell's office with telegrams and phone calls. A few nights later, when Campbell and his secretary attended the Deroit-Montreal game at the Montreal Forum, both were assaulted with epithets and rotten eggs and tomatoes. Though the two teams were locked in a struggle for first place, and this game was a crucial one in the race, the crowd seemed unable to concentrate on the game. Before the second period was to begin, a smoke bomb exploded, filling the Forum with searing fumes. The fans poured into the streets outside, where a mob of ten thousand formed and pillaged the surrounding area. Cab drivers were pulled from their autos and beaten. Rocks and bottles flew. Windows were smashed and stores looted. Newsstands were overturned and burned. It was three in the morning before the police had quelled the rampage.

News of the riot made headlines across the western world. In London, one newspaper editorialized, "Ice hockey is rough, but it is now a matter of record that Canadian players are spring lambs compared to those who support them."

Today, hockey is actually less violent than it was twenty years ago, when team and individual feuds erupted in stick-swinging duels and bench-clearing brawls. "Those games," recalls Frank Udvari, a former NHL referee who is now the league's Eastern Supervisor of Officials, "were wars compared to what they are today."

If pro hockey violence appears to be on the increase, it is primarily because the sport is covered more extensively than ever before for an ever-increasing audience. Since the major expansion in 1967, pro hockey has become a nationally televised sport and generated a seemingly endless stream of books and magazines. The home and away games of most teams are carried on radio and reported in the local newspapers, and the road games of many are televised. Yet the expanded coverage has tended to be simplistic. American sportswriters and sports commentators, who are more familiar with the games they have played and watched since childhood, have suddenly had to become experts on a game relatively new to them. Naturally, they have been quick to

More defiant than uncomfortable, part of the
Forum crowd celebrates the smoke-bomb explosion
that precipitated the clearing of the arena
and the subsequent Richard Riot outside.

notice and stress its obviously violent nature, without realizing that hockey's historically rugged standards of violence are slipping. In the rush to cover hockey's latest incident of brutality, the media have rarely put the event in historical perspective.

For example, it is rarely mentioned outside hockey circles that there are simply more pro games today. "It's a simple case of arithmetic," says Punch Imlach, general manager of the Buffalo Sabres. "Whenever you build a new arena you increase the chances of an incident. There are eighteen teams in the NHL. Only a few years ago there were six. Consequently, the chances of something ugly happening should have tripled."

Hockey's ugly incidents have been much publicized, perhaps even overemphasized. After decades of being ignored outside Canada, the game is learning that publicity has its price. Yet to ignore or placidly accept hockey's excesses is as much a misrepresentation as to harp on them, for hockey has not solved the problem of excessive violence and has been reluctant to address its root causes. Meanwhile, the problems of the pro game have permeated the amateur leagues it fosters.

In hockey's perhaps most tragic incident in recent years, Paul Smithers, a 17-year-old who was one of the few black players in Canadian amateur hockey, was convicted of manslaughter in the death of an opposing player after an amateur hockey game in Applewood, Ontario, in 1973. Testimony revealed that the victim, Barrie Ross Cobby, had subjected Smithers and his family to numerous racial slurs during the game, provoking both teams and even the crowd into a brawl that eventually spilled into the parking lot outside.

"The inevitable explosion came when Smithers followed Cobby outside the arena to the parking lot, determined to get an apology or a fight," reported a story in the New York *Times.* "Smithers punched Cobby once and was then grabbed by four Applewood players. With his arms and neck pinned, he kicked out instinctively as Cobby lunged toward him. Cobby crumpled to the ground, clutching his groin. Minutes later he was dead, choked on his own vomit." (The parents of the dead boy contested much of the *Times* story and the court testimony, but there was no contesting the gruesome outcome of the incident.)

A year later, in the 1974 playoffs, the president of the Bramalea Blues Junior B team, Gerry Henderson, withdrew his team from competition against the Hamilton Red Wings in Hamilton. Henderson said he actually feared for the lives of his players during a brawl in which almost 200 minutes in penalties were called, and a dozen extra policemen were required to restore order on the ice and in the stands. For his actions, Henderson was suspended for two years by the Ontario Hockey Association.

As a result of the incident, the Minister of Community and Social Services for the Province of Ontario directed a Toronto attorney, William R. McMurtry, to hold a full-scale investigation into violence in amateur hockey. Over a three-month period, McMurtry interviewed social scientists, sports psychologists, educators, and experts in physical fitness and recreation, as well as former and current players, coaches, and officials in professional and amateur hockey.

"After completing my investigation and research," McMurtry reported, "I believe it is possible to determine with some degree of certainty the actual causes of violence in amateur hockey."

Among the causes McMurtry listed were:

(1) Influence of professional hockey (particularly the NHL) and its emphasis on winning and the use of violence as a tactical instrument to achieve that goal.

(2) A rule structure (in professional and amateur hockey) which not only tolerates but encourages the use of violence by rewarding those who excel at physical intimidation.

"The influence has been compounded with the advent of television," McMurtry continued. "Professional sport, by its very nature, dominates the mass media in its quest for spectators. Now the images presented by TV dwarf the effect of home and school in the minds of most sports-conscious youngsters. . . .

"In talking to numerous players in the NHL and WHA, they all feel that most advertising and selling of the game is overemphasizing the fighting and brawling at the expense of educating the crowds about the skill and finesse. This past season [1973–74], the advertising for the NBC Game of the Week showed a film clip of a hockey fight. . . . The much-heralded 'Peter Puck' cartoon series designed to educate the American fan as to the intricacies of the game is a case in point. In every segment the players were characterized as brutal, top-

The 1974–75 season began with the Flyers and Seals brawling in Oakland, *below,* and ended with Dave Williams and Dave Hutchison swinging sticks in L.A., *opposite.* Clarence Campbell called it the NHL's "worst year ever for sheer violence."

heavy, Neanderthal types who were shown demonstrating every conceivable type of foul with great gusto.''

In the 1974–75 season, the NHL experienced its "worst year ever for sheer violence on the ice," according to Campbell. With the season only two weeks old, a Flyers-Seals game in Oakland erupted in a near riot. In midseason came the much-publicized Forbes-Boucha case (see Chapter 2). By season's end a slew of brawling, stick swinging, and other outbreaks had caused Campbell to dispense some of the stiffest punishment in years. Los Angeles' Dave Hutchison and Toronto's Dave Williams received suspensions for a stick-swinging duel in the opening round of the playoffs. Bob Plager, a defenseman for the St. Louis Blues, assaulted referee Andy Van Hellemond after the final playoff game between the Blues and the Penguins, sending the referee to the hospital for 10 days and earning a five-game suspension.

No sooner had Campbell issued the last of his disciplinary measures than the Philadelphia Flyers won their second straight Stanley Cup, prompting many coaches and general managers to examine Philadelphia coach Fred Shero's much-vaunted "system," an integral part of which is the tactical use of fouling (see Chapter 3).

The violent game is not a new story, but the events of 1974–75 proved once again that it continues to be a topical one.

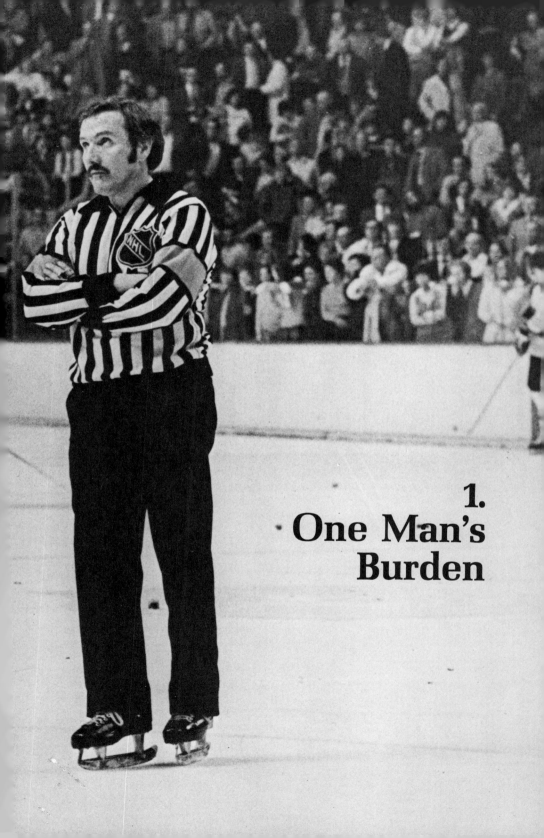

1.
One Man's Burden

By the late afternoon of Sunday, May 19, the 1974 Stanley Cup playoffs had reached their climax. Before 17,000 roaring fans at the Spectrum in Philadelphia and millions watching on television, the Philadelphia Flyers and Boston Bruins had culminated their duel for hockey's greatest prize with 57 minutes of nonstop action. At stake were $15,000 per man and the honor and prestige of winning the oldest, most revered sports trophy in North America.

Going into this, the most important game of the year, the Flyers were leading in the series by three games to two. One more victory and they would become the first expansion team in National Hockey League history to win the Stanley Cup. The brash, boisterous team that had established new penalty records and been denounced as a band of untalented bullies had won the NHL's West Division. Now it was on the verge of ultimate vindication.

After winning the East Division and leading the league in scoring for the seventh year in a row, the Bruins had been stunned by the hungry Flyers, dropping three of the first four games. Three nights before, in Boston Garden, the Bruins had responded to possible elimination with their finest effort of the series, drubbing the Flyers 5–1. Another victory for the Bruins would force a seventh and deciding game back in Boston, where the Flyers had managed to win only twice in seven years. "Tell the Flyers they don't have to take all that champagne back to Philadelphia," Bruins coach Bep Guidolin chortled after the fifth game, remembering the cases of bubbly the Flyers had chilled in their dressing room before the game. "They can leave it here and we'll drink it for them Tuesday."

With so much at stake in game six, one might have expected a defensive, low-risk game, at least at the start. But from the opening whistle, both teams skated furiously and developed some solid scoring opportunities. The goaltending, however, was impeccable and, with one notable exception, unbeatable. The breach came at 14:49 of the first period, when Rick MacLeish of the Flyers tipped a shot past Gilles Gilbert, in goal for Boston.

The Bruins answered with brilliant assaults on Philadelphia goalie Bernie Parent, yet as the game entered the final three minutes of regulation play, Boston had failed to convert. The scoreboard clock high above center ice was ticking away the final minutes, and the one-goal Philadelphia lead loomed greater than ever.

The call that killed the Bruins. With only two minutes left in the final game of the 1974 Stanley Cup playoffs, Art Skov sends Bruins' Bobby Orr off for holding Flyers' Bobby Clarke on a breakaway.

With two and a half minutes left, the pressing Bruins were caught critically off guard. Parent made a fine kick save on a shot by Boston's Ken Hodge. Suddenly, the puck caromed out of the Philadelphia zone into center ice, where the Flyers' irrepressible Bobby Clarke gath-

ered it in and started toward the Boston zone on a break-away. As Clarke swept across the blue line, only the Bruins' magnificent Bobby Orr had a chance to catch him. Orr charged at Clarke from the side, reached him, and in a desperate attempt to prevent him from shooting, flung his right arm and stick around Clarke's waist, spinning him around and dragging him to the ice about fifteen feet from the net.

Immediately, the right arm of referee Art Skov shot into the air, signaling a penalty on the Bruins. With 2:22 left, Orr headed for the penalty box to serve two minutes for holding. Boston's hopes of coming back to win the Stanley Cup went with him. The Bruins were forced to play all but the final 22 seconds of the game not only shorthanded but without their best player.

Was it a foul? There was no doubt in Skov's mind. "I was in a position to see what Orr did to Clarke," the referee says. "I was off to the left of the play and I saw Orr's right arm come across in front of Clarke. But I also saw him grab Clarke's left arm with his left hand and jerk him around. From the angle I had, it was an obvious penalty." Few objective observers disagreed. Indeed, it is possible that if Skov erred in any way, it was on the side of leniency. "Some people even felt that Clarke could have been given a penalty shot," Skov reports.

It seemed like an obvious foul, but Skov's call was a courageous one nevertheless. At the very least it forced the players and fans to stop and accept his critically important judgment at the most heated point of the game, when the players themselves would normally have been the sole object of attention. A referee knows that fans do not pay up to twelve dollars a ticket to watch him make difficult decisions that stop the action. They would much rather watch a hockey game in which the flow and excitement are uninterrupted. They tolerate whistles to the extent that they order the play. But when the whistles begin to rule rather than regulate the play, the fans get restless. And when a call is made that drastically and dramatically alters, or threatens to alter, the outcome of a contest—as Skov's did—there is bound to be some disapproval, no matter how justified the call.

Referees are remembered for the calls they make, rarely for the calls they miss. The flow of a hockey game can wash away the memory of even the flagrant fouls, provided that they are not highlighted by a referee's call. When they are, the play stops, the offender is dramatically banished, the foul is entered in the record, and, of course, a power play ensues. Would-be second-guessers follow the next two minutes of play intensely aware of the call that shaped them. Later, critics can review the record, point to the penalty, and speculate on what effect it had on the game.

A missed foul causes no dramatic play stoppage, no notation in the record, and, of course, no power play. In the words of the hockey announcer, "Play carries on," and so does the attention of the crowd. There may be a momentary howl of protest, but there is no time for more. Later, there may be some residual grumbling about a ref missing one, but it is difficult to remember specifics. It's much easier to dwell on the ones he did call.

Because a referee's job is to minimize controversy, not create it, he likes to be certain, when he makes a call as important as Skov's, not only that he has spotted a foul, but also that the foul deserves a whistle. As the Orr-Clarke situation demonstrated, a two-minute minor penalty with two minutes to play can have the effect of

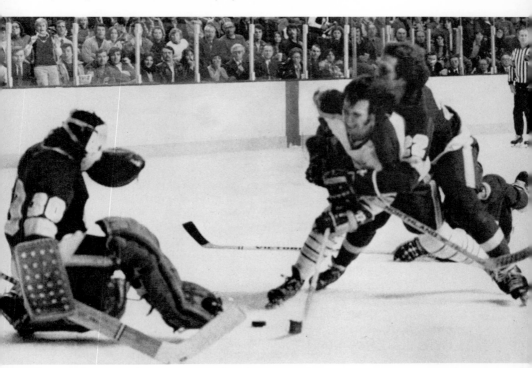

A good penalty. Without the clutch of Kings' Barry Long, Sabres' Rick Dudley would be in alone on goal. Note referee out of position.

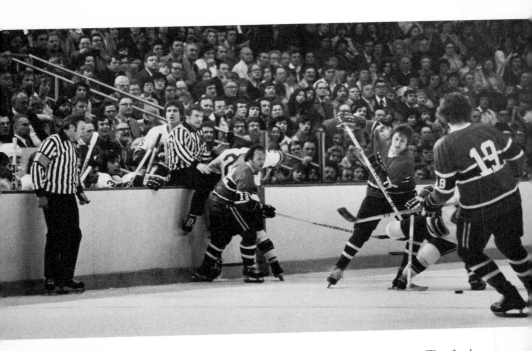

a match penalty at the beginning of the game. The foul had better merit such punishment. In this case, Orr illegally denied Clarke an excellent chance to ice the game, so it was not unreasonable to call a penalty that, in effect, did the same.

Hockey people often make a distinction between "good" and "bad" penalties. A "good penalty" is a foul that serves a clearly worthwhile purpose—most often to prevent a score. A "bad penalty" is a foul that is of little help, and certainly not worth two minutes. Referees also recognize this difference. Moreover, they may rely on it in deciding whether or not to step in at a crucial point in the game. Lloyd Gilmour, a senior NHL referee and the man who would have officiated the seventh Flyers-Bruins game had it taken place, says, "What I call in the third period may differ completely from what I'll call in the first or second period. Why? Because of the score, mostly. Maybe that's not the way it should be, but it is. For example, I'll probably call a trip in the neutral zone in the first period. But in the last three minutes of the game, with the score tied or a one-goal difference, I'll only call what the players refer to as 'good penalties.'"

Top and *left:* A bad penalty. Murray Wilson, center, commits a center-ice trip in front of referee Lloyd Gilmour. The call is obvious. *Opposite:* Clearing the crease. Interference or incidental pushing and shoving?

"With a few minutes to go and the score tied, or a one-goal difference, you don't want the game decided on a cheap penalty," declares Philadelphia coach Fred Shero. "If you trip a man to save a goal and the trip is flagrant, the referee should call it. But if the man is taking a dive, or if the referee isn't sure, he should overlook it. I don't want to win a game on a cheap penalty—that doesn't do anything for me. And I want the same consideration when my team is out there trying to protect a one-goal lead."

There are other situations too in which the referee tailors his interpretation of fouls to the climate of the game. For example, if two teams have a history of bad blood between them, a referee may elect to crack down early, calling even marginal violations, in an effort to show that he is in charge. On the other hand, if two teams are playing a free-wheeling contest with a minimum of infractions, a referee may overlook even a particularly obvious foul, hoping not to destroy the flow of an essentially well-played game. The rule book becomes merely a guide, and sometimes not even that. Bill Chadwick, the former great referee, says that because each

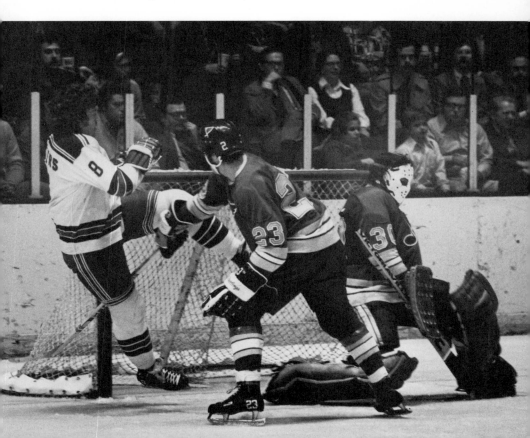

game has a different character, a referee is well advised at times to forget the rule book and concentrate on making his rulings fit the character of the game.

Almost to a man, referees and their supervisors say that if they called a game by following the rule book literally there would be no game at all. "If I called interference the way it appears in the rule book, I'd be calling it thirty or forty times a game," says Bill Friday, a long-time NHL referee now the senior official in the World Hockey Association. "Just about every time one winger shadows another winger, he's interfering with him if you interpret it literally. Not to mention what goes on in front of the net when the defensemen are trying to clear and the forwards are trying for a shot or a rebound."

Despite all the good intentions, however, the practice of policing a hockey game simply by trusting the referee to see all the fouls and interpret the rule book appropriately can have unpleasant consequences. Violent fouling is one of them.

Even the most mature referee with the most finely

tuned feel for controlling a game cannot call what he cannot see. Skating up the ice behind a rapidly developing rush, he is likely to miss what goes on behind him, or even far ahead of him. When players pile up in the corners, he is likely to be shielded from the more vicious infighting. Even when he has an unobstructed view of a foul, he may miss it simply because he is looking the other way. For example, while a scramble for the puck goes on in a corner or along the sideboards and the referee follows the play, a defenseman may be illegally slashing or dumping an opposing forward in front of the net. It happens frequently and is often missed. Pittsburgh's Steve Durbano admits, "If someone's trying to park himself in front of our net, I'll whack him across the ankles when the puck goes into the corner and I'm sure the referee isn't looking."

Moreover, even the best referees are caught out of position. Says Skov, "You do your best to be in position, but the game is so fast you don't always succeed. . . . If I had been to the right of the [Orr-Clarke] play, I wouldn't have seen what Orr did with his left-hand. From there it might even have looked as if Clarke took a dive—I don't know."

Frank Udvari, formerly a great referee, now a super-

Clear fouls don't always draw a call. Even if the referee has a good angle on the play, he may simply not react quickly enough. *Opposite:* Cross-check; *above:* slash.

visor of officials in the NHL, says that he saw 96 to 98 percent of what went on in games he refereed. But he too acknowledges that the angle at which he saw plays had an important bearing on whether he called a penalty. He remembers a game in the early fifties when the Canadiens' Ken Mosdell rounded the net with an opposing forward. Suddenly, the forward went down. On the other side of the net from the play, Udvari saw the man go down but couldn't be sure why. So he called nothing, following the referee's dictum—"If you don't know, don't blow."

But when the play recurred later, he broke out of position and raced behind the net with Mosdell. This time he caught the Canadien red-handed, dumping his man with a subtle but effective spear. Udvari whistled him off. However, Mosdell apparently still believed he could get away with this trick. Later in the game he tried it a third time. This time Udvari kept his normal position, straddling the goal line on the other side of the

Hugging the goal line, referee is in best possible position to see play in the defensive zone, but he can be screened. Here he may have lost sight of the puck, though it is still very much in play.

net. Down went the opposing forward; up went Udvari's right arm. He hadn't seen the spear, but he'd seen enough of the play to know there had been one. (That convinced Mosdell. He didn't utter a syllable of protest.) Using his experience and some initiative, Udvari caught two of Mosdell's three fouls, even though he was twice in a position to see only the result of the foul, not the foul itself.

How many fouls does the average referee miss during a game? Naturally, it varies. In a relatively orderly contest, with none of the players out to provoke, intimidate, or retaliate, there are likely to be few fouls and the referee may miss none of them. If he does miss one, it may not matter. But in a game in which passions run high and little is required to incite a player into avenging some real or imagined affront, fouls are likely to proliferate. A referee is bound to miss one, and then an escalating chain of violence becomes inevitable.

"There's a certain amount of retaliation involved in the game," says Dan Maloney of the Detroit Red Wings. "When you're on the ice and playing aggressively, and hitting hard, when tempers are really flaring and you get hooked or elbowed, it makes you so mad you lash out."

Buffalo's Rick Martin remembers that when the Flyers' Ed Van Impe fouled to keep up with him, "I put a bead on his head with two shots. One hit him in the chest. He didn't bother me after that."

"There's always a reason when hockey players fight," says Shero. "Maybe just previous to the fight a man was slashed unnecessarily, or high-sticked, or butt-ended by an opponent, only the referee didn't see it. Or didn't call it. If a man keeps taking this, he's going to be run out of the league. He's got to defend himself."

The trouble is that what seems like just getting even to one man is considered a challenge and a putdown by another. Both may be afraid of "getting run out of the league." Both may intend only to defend themselves. But each defends himself in a way that the other interprets as a threat. It is a syndrome older than hockey, and it unfolds hundreds of times in a season. And it is complicated by the fact that there are hockey players who really are trying to run others out of the league, and still other players who probably can be run out. Intimidation can play a major role in determining who wins and who loses a game (see Chapter 3).

If the best way to intimidate another player is by

fouling him—especially if the referee is looking elsewhere—the best way to prove one can't be intimidated is retaliation in kind. Soon the battle is on.

Perhaps the most horrifying example of such escalating violence was the confrontation in September, 1968, in Ottawa, Canada, between Ted Green of the Boston Bruins and Wayne Maki of the St. Louis Blues. It did not take place during the sixth game of the Stanley Cup finals, or even in a regular-season contest, but during a meaningless exhibition game. Maki was a young forward trying to make the St. Louis club. Green was a veteran defenseman who had thrived on his reputation as one of the NHL's fiercest players.

After about 13 minutes of a dull first period, the puck caromed behind the Bruins' net with both Green and Maki in pursuit. While scuffling for possession, Maki grabbed Green by the back of the sweater. Green promptly shoved his glove into Maki's face, and Maki answered by ramming his stick into Green's stomach. Incensed at what he interpreted as a deliberate attempt to injure by spearing, Green brought his stick down on Maki's shoulder. Maki then swung back with his stick, the heel of its blade thudding against the right side of Green's head. Green sank to the ice, his head grotesquely twisted. Saliva oozed from the corner of his mouth, blood flowed from a cut near his right temple.

The entire incident had taken less than 15 seconds.

Green was rushed to the hospital, where it was discovered that skull fragments had been driven through the tough membrane encasing his brain, paralyzing the entire left side of his body. Over the next few months, surgeons performed three delicate operations on Green's brain. In one, they inserted a plate in his skull. The doctors predicted that his hockey career was over—indeed, he was fortunate to be alive, they said.

The viciousness of the duel and its ugly consequences made front-page news across North America. In the heat of editorial comment deploring the NHL's failure to police itself, Ottawa police served warrants on Maki and Green for "assault causing bodily harm." The players stood trial separately.

Before Judge Edward Carter, Maki explained that he had been "frightened" by Green. "I once saw Green give it [his stick] to Doug Mohns of Chicago," Maki said, "and he would have killed him if Doug hadn't been wearing a helmet."

Bobby Clarke and Tim Horton demonstrate how a fight begins: cross-check, high stick, and confrontation.

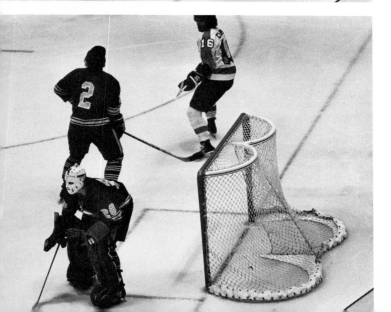

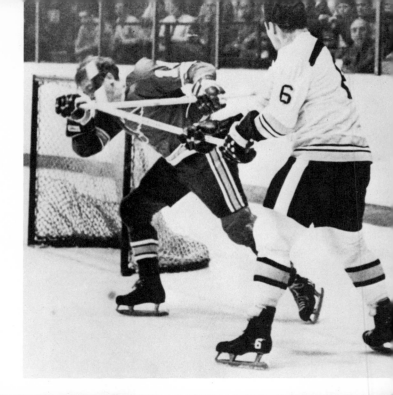

The judge found Maki not guilty, explaining that he believed Maki to have been "under reasonable apprehension of bodily harm." The judge concluded, "If no doubt was raised in my mind of self-defense, Maki would have been guilty."

A different judge, Michael J. Fitzpatrick, found Green not guilty for very similar reasons. He made the point that "neither the referee nor either of the linesmen made any reference to any spearing that may have been taking place on the boards; but there are competent witnesses . . . who were there who state that while the two players were scuffling along the boards Mr. Maki made a spearing motion, jabbed at Mr. Green, with the blade of his stick in the lower abdomen. . . .

"It is interesting to note that Mr. Maki has no memory of this having happened. He does not remember spearing Mr. Green. But I note from his evidence that he was quite careful to say that he does not say that he did not spear him; he just does not remember. . . .

"Mr. Green also said that when he had been speared, as he said, in the testicles by Mr. Maki, he then struck him a sort of half chop on the shoulder as a warning not to do it again, to desist. . . . I have no doubt . . . that the blow struck by Mr. Green was almost immediately after the blow—the much more serious blow in my opinion, the spearing—which had been struck at him by Mr. Maki. I do not think that Mr. Green was doing anything more in the circumstances than protecting himself."

In short, the judges could not agree on which man had been the aggressor. Each judge believed that the man before him had been defending himself—and each judge may have been right. Perhaps if there had been only one trial, either Green or Maki would have been found guilty, but it is likely that justice was better served by the separate trials. Each man truly believed that he was defending himself even while committing a horrendous act. The hockey code of protective reaction had produced a grisly duel in which neither man was truly culpable.

Another significant aspect of the case was that neither Green nor Maki heeded the referee's call before retaliating. As it happened, the referee missed Maki's spearing, but signaled for a two-minute penalty on Green for slashing. Neither man responded.

In ice hockey, more than in any other sport, excessive fouling *is expected* to redress players' grievances

The tragedy of retaliation. After being speared by Wayne Maki, Ted Green retaliates with a chopping blow, *opposite top*, provoking Maki into the slash, *opposite bottom*, that almost killed Green.

against other players. A brushback pitch in baseball, an elbow in the face in basketball, a knee in the groin in football all provoke retaliation. Then the referee steps in and at least controls, if he does not eliminate, the abuses. In hockey, one slash leads to another, and sometimes, before the referee and his linesmen can react, the situation is beyond control.

In large part, the key to preventing fouls of violence is earning the players' confidence that the provocative fouls will be caught and penalized. If the referee can do that, there is a good chance that the victimized player will not feel obliged to retaliate. But if the original foul is missed—or, even more important, if he expects it to be missed—then the victimized player feels little reason to restrain himself. Indeed, he feels he has to respond.

"It's not what you lose by backing off from that first reef in the back," says Sid Abel, the former Red Wings star, now the general manager of the Kansas City Scouts. "It's what's going to happen to you down the road if you *don't* retaliate. The word spreads like wildfire, and when it gets around that you can be intimidated, forget it. You're going to have everybody in the league taking shots at you, even the nonviolent types."

Even when the referees see fouls, there are sometimes other considerations that seem to influence their calls and outweigh their commitment to preventing more violence. Perhaps the most important is their tendency to "even up" the penalties they call. Hockey referees are often criticized for an alleged inconsistency in the types of fouls they call, and according to the players, they seem to regard evening up the calls as their best defense. The Islanders' Denis Potvin says, "The referees are striving for what the league refers to as consistency. That's how they are rated and judged. Consistency, according to the NHL, is giving out roughly an equal number of penalties to each team."

If the referee can't see all the fouls and can't call all the ones he does see, his next best alternative is to distribute equally the ones he does call. Evening up the calls, whether or not they are consistent, strengthens his image of impartiality. The NHL cites the relatively small discrepancy in penalties against the different teams as proof of the referees' fairness.

If the level of fouling between two teams is equal, evening up the calls does not prevent the referee from being both consistent and impartial. He can set a stan-

dard of foul calling, confident that the penalties that result and the fouls he lets go will naturally fall about
equally between the two clubs. Unfortunately, fouls don't
always even up, and when they don't, evening up the
foul *calls* ceases to be either even-handed or consistent.

Evening up the foul calls is probably an unconscious
policy of the referees. They operate under great pressure, partly because the calls they make or fail to make
affect the game more than those of officials in other
sports. For example, in pro basketball, a two-shot foul
call in favor of a team that averages a 75 percent foul-
shooting percentage and 100 points a game will, on the
average, result in 1.5 points, or 1.5 percent of the team's
score. In hockey, a foul call in favor of a team that scores
on 20 percent of its power plays and averages 3 goals
a game will, on the average, result in .2 goals, or 6.6
percent of its average score. Thus, a foul call in basketball is about four and a half times less important than
one in hockey, which may explain why there are so many
more of them. In any case, the reluctance of hockey referees to call too many fouls, and their tendency to even
up the ones they do call, encourage the escalation of
violent fouling. The message is simple: the more consistently and more violently a team fouls, the more it is
likely to get away with.

Another extra consideration of the referees is their
favoring of the home team. There is evidence to suggest
that visiting teams may be penalized more stringently
than home teams, and that this encourages the syndrome of challenging and intimidating that leads to un-
necessary, violent, often dangerous fouling.

Hockey followers have long recognized a "home-
ice" advantage. Traditionally, a team is happy to break
even on the road. It is expected to—and usually does—
make most of its points at home. No one is certain about
what accounts for the home team's advantage, but few
people dispute its existence. In 1973–74, every team had
a better record at home than on the road—most teams
were dramatically better. In 1972–73 and 1973–74, home
teams won a total of 675 games and lost only 382, a winning percentage of .638. The comparable figure in basketball was .607, in football .584, and in baseball .532.

This at-home advantage, the greatest in the four
major team sports, is usually laid to any or all of three
factors: the home team being inspired by the crowd, the
home club's greater familiarity with its rink, and/or its

38

greater rest from lack of travel. They are all plausible explanations, but even cumulatively they do not fully explain the home-ice advantage.

If it were true that the home team gained an advantage from its familiarity with the rink and from greater rest, then one would expect that advantage to have increased since expansion. Today, there are three times as many teams as there were in 1966–67, and the travel demands have become brutal. From a relatively compact league of three Eastern teams (Montreal, Boston, and New York), and three Midwestern clubs (Toronto, Detroit, and Chicago), the NHL has become a nationwide

Philadelphia fan approves the referee's verdict. Hometown pressures, particularly in Philadelphia, are rarely so polite.

circuit, with two teams on the West Coast, and one in the Deep South. The original six teams visited five rinks seven times each. Today's teams visit seventeen rinks no more than three times each. Nevertheless, the home team advantage has not changed much since pre-expansion days. For the two seasons 1965–66 and 1966–67 (the last two before expansion), the home team won 226 games and lost 136, a .624 winning percentage, or about 1.4 percent less than today's home teams.

No doubt hockey teams, especially young ones, are often inspired by their supporters and rattled by the pressure in alien rinks, but this factor is not unique to hockey. Football teams have even more to gain or lose from the momentum that cheering creates. A driving football team controls the game more than a driving hockey team because it is far easier to control a football than a hockey puck. In football, one team has possession of the ball, and if it executes its plays with the spirit a crowd can give it, it is not likely to surrender the ball before scoring. In hockey, possession of the puck is constantly shifting, and even if one team can control the puck and set up its plays perfectly, it may still be foiled by the goalie. In short, momentum inspired by the home crowd would seem to count more in football than in hockey, yet the home-team advantage is significantly greater in hockey.

A far more telling explanation of the home-ice advantage is the refereeing, which tends to favor a team that is trailing and a team that has just been scored on, particularly if it is the home team.

In New York Rangers games in 1973–74, there were 461 penalties called that resulted in power plays. The Rangers had 222, or 48.2 percent of the power plays, compared to 239, or 51.8 percent, for their opponents. Of the power plays when the Rangers were winning, the Rangers had 43.2 percent. When the Rangers were winning on the road, their share of power plays dropped further, to 28 percent. However, when the Rangers were winning at home, it rose to 51.1 percent. In other words, when the Rangers were winning at home they had a 33.1 percent greater share of the power plays than when they were winning on the road.

Of the power plays that followed a Rangers score, the Rangers had only 37 percent overall. At home the figure rose to 44 percent, whereas on the road it fell to 24.5 percent, a difference of 20.4 percent. Of the power plays that followed an opponent's score, the Rangers had a 24 percent greater share at home than on the road.

In the case of the 1974–75 Philadelphia Flyers, there was no significant difference between the Flyers' share of the power plays at home and on the road after a Flyers' score. But after an opponent's score, the Flyers had a 32.3 percent greater share of the power plays at home than on the road. (See Appendix for complete statistics on 1973–74 Rangers and 1974–75 Flyers.)

Taken as a whole the statistics suggest that, for whatever reason, referees have a tendency to "compensate" when one team is winning or when one team scores. And they do more compensating if the beneficiary is the home team. The home-ice advantage is not, it seems, as intangible as the inspiration that comes from the roar of the crowd.

At Boston Garden on March 11, 1975, in a game between the Bruins and Rangers, referee Andy Van Hellemond called three penalties on the Bruins and none on the Rangers in the second period. In the third period he called no penalties until five minutes remained. Then, with the score tied 3–3 and the Bruins pressing for the win, Phil Esposito tried to break from his defensive zone after a loose puck in center ice. Rangers rookie defenseman Ron Greschner, who was caught out of position, obstructed Esposito's progress until a Ranger could recover the puck. When the Boston center freed himself from Greschner, he raised his stick and rapped the defenseman with it.

Van Hellemond called Greschner for interference, but he made no call on Esposito. On the ensuing power play, the Bruins scored the game-winning goal. The Rangers were incensed. At the very least, they claimed, Esposito should also have been penalized.

Aside from the merits of the call, many knowledgeable observers routinely interpreted it as a hometown decision. A Boston player would not have been penalized for doing what Greschner did, it was said, especially since the Bruins had already taken three penalties in a row. Moreover, it was assumed that Greschner would not have been penalized had the game been in New York.

Hockey players, as well as most other people connected with the sport, are often reluctant to explicitly link a home-ice advantage to the referee's decisions. Yet it is commonly accepted around the league that hometown crowds do "call" penalties for referees, particularly in Philadelphia and Buffalo. In Philadelphia, in the seventh game of the Flyers-Islanders 1975 semifinal playoff series, a particularly questionable tripping call on Denis Potvin of the Islanders late in the game reportedly provoked the following exchange between Islanders goalie Glenn Resch and referee Lloyd Gilmour.

Resch: Mr. Gilmour, you're an experienced referee. Don't you know the difference between a trip and a dive?

Gilmour: Yes, I do, and it's going to stop pretty soon.

Resch: Well, you *better* stop it pretty soon, 'cause we're running out of time.

Trailing 3–1 after the opening minutes of the game, the Islanders were plagued in their catch-up bid by a

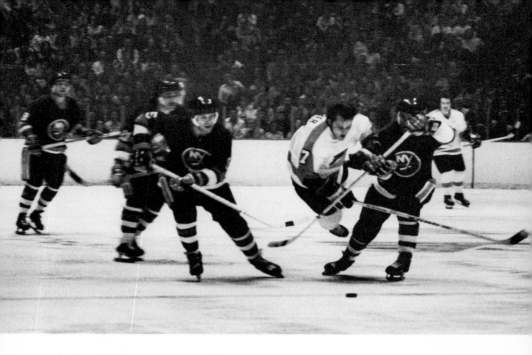

half dozen penalties, many of which the television replay showed to have been called for nonexistent fouls. The Islanders never did catch up.

No matter what they attribute it to, all hockey teams believe in the advantage of playing at home, and adjust their strategy accordingly. A team generally plays with more assurance at home. It takes more chances. Instead of sitting on a lead it is likely to try to break the game open. Of the more than 200 games in 1973–74 decided by 3 goals or more, the home team won 72 percent. On the road a team generally plays more conservatively, afraid of being caught out of position.

In terms of fouling, especially flagrant fouling intended to intimidate, the home team is expected to be more daring. It is much more likely to feel that it can afford an early penalty, or even an early score against it, if in the process it can establish its physical superiority over the opposition.

In addition, there are players who feel the need to be more aggressive at home, in an attempt to build a good reputation among the fans. Says Ted Lindsay, the former terror of the Detroit Red Wings and now a television broadcaster, "There are a lot of guys who . . . feel that if they can intimidate you in front of the hometown fans . . . they'll become heroes."

It is even accepted around the league that there

A trip or a dive? Bill Barber flies through
the air with the greatest of ease
while Islanders provide pretext of a foul.

are players who will fight only at home. In his book *The Broad Street Bullies,* Philadelphia hockey writer Jack Chevalier quotes Flyers bad boy Dave Schultz on why he scored more at the Spectrum than on the road in 1973–74. " 'There's not as many chances to fight here [in Philadelphia],' said Schultz, 'because when I challenge guys they back off.' "

If players accepted a system of intimidating at home and being intimidated on the road, there would not be such an incentive for violent fouling. But obviously, many do not accept it. A visiting team knows that, other things being equal, it is the underdog when it enters the rink. It is challenged to prove its moxie, particularly if the home side has a reputation for roughing up visitors. Quite justifiably, the visitors feel that unless they stand up to the hometown boys, they risk being run out of the rink. It is a challenge especially hard for the game's bad guys to ignore. Says Abel of Ted Lindsay, "He really got jacked up on the road. He was a better player on the road than at home because he felt the odds were against him there."

The refereeing does nothing to allay these fears. Rather, it contributes to them by contributing to the home-ice advantage, which teams realize they must overcome to win. As of now, they have the unhappy choice of moving immediately to combat the threat of home-team intimidation or laying back and accepting the abuse. If they choose to be belligerent, they risk penalties that may lead to scores against them that they cannot afford. If they choose to be passive, the visitors rely on the vain hope that with the referee's help they can survive. The choice is to be penalized by the referee for protecting yourself or by the aggressors for failing to.

Confronted with such a choice, most teams will opt for belligerence and challenge the referee to crack down.

At the Spectrum on February 6, 1975, the Rangers and Flyers began fighting 13 seconds after the opening faceoff, virtually without a check having been thrown. The Flyers had beaten the Rangers the night before in New York, and were now expected to run roughshod over them in Philadelphia. Clearly, the Rangers felt it necessary to show they were not about to be bullied at the Spectrum. Rookie John Bednarski immediately collided with Dave Schultz, and the battle began.

The New York *Post* reported, "Though the Flyers were more often vicious aggressors, the Rangers were not blameless. As a team often accused of not playing dirty enough in a sport where violence not only helps sell tickets but has become an integral part of the strategy, the Rangers' honor and pride was at stake.

"The first period lasted one hour as players from both teams fought, grappled, cursed, and menaced one another on the ice . . . Confusion and chaos prevailed. Orderly control of the game was impossible."

Both teams seemed to consider the brawling an unpleasant but necessary part of the game. Said the Rangers' captain, Brad Park, "We weren't going to take any —— from them."

Said the Flyers' Don Saleski, "The Rangers showed me something they haven't shown before . . . courage."

Most hockey games do not follow this pattern. There are many deterrents to fouls of violence, more today than ever before. One traditionally powerful deterrent is the score and the game situation. Hardly anyone is senseless enough to want to take a penalty when it might cost the game.

But there are also new incentives to foul. In the old six-team league, most home teams didn't dare take too many liberties with visitors because they knew that they would soon (often the next night) have to play in the visitor's rink. The teams had 14 meetings in which they evolved a brutal but fairly stable balance of fouling. They were enemies but they were also neighbors who, in a sense, had to live in each other's homes.

Sid Abel recalls, "Those Saturday night games in Montreal, then Sunday night games back in Detroit, they were part of the game that doesn't exist today. When we'd go into Montreal, we'd almost *dare* them to start something, because we knew we'd have them back in the Olympia less than twenty-four hours later. They talk about a home-ice advantage, well there really wasn't much of one then because we always knew that we would be getting them back in our rink while everyone's memory was fresh. You didn't have time to forget what someone did to you. It was on your mind when you went on the ice in Detroit."

Today, a home team is virtually free of this constraint. By the time it repays a visit, months may have gone by, and the animosities (in some cases even the players) may have been dropped. The next confrontation is just too far in the future to be a deterrent.

This is one change in the game's pattern of fouling

44

to which the refereeing has not adapted. It still favors the home club, encouraging both the home team and the visitors to foul.

Perhaps it was the Canadian G. E. Mortimer who best described the plight of the man whose job it is to police the furiously fast, violent game of pro hockey. Mortimer likened the NHL referee to "a strong, respected frontier sheriff, keeping order by arresting a few men here and there as examples, while knowing that hot-tempered gunmen will shoot it out when his back is turned; sometimes in front of him."

Like the frontier sheriff, the NHL referee is respected by the players and tolerated by the fans as long as he

doesn't perform his constable's function too assiduously. Fans like to see action and players like to produce it, and neither want the referee to interfere. Yet when the action gets out of hand, both look to the agent of law to do something. He responds by trying desperately to see all the fouls so as to be better able to decide which of them to let go. But when he fails, as any human being inevitably will, he subconsciously reconciles himself to treating the symptoms of discontent rather than their cause, evening up the calls with a slight advantage for the home team in a final, inevitably feeble, attempt to make everyone happy—or at least not too unhappy. It's an unsatisfactory but hardly surprising fate for an agent of law in a land of disorder.

Man of law in a land of disorder, referee Art Skov, right, knows better than to try to quell the chaos.

2.
The Cost

Montreal's Guy Lafleur was winding up for one of his lightning rushes. He picked up the puck in the Canadiens' zone, and by the time he reached his blue line, the little right winger was flying. He flitted past his check, Toronto's Darryl Sittler. The frustrated Sittler whirled about, lifted his stick, and with both hands brought it cracking down across Lafleur's hands. Looking ahead at the rapidly developing play, Lafleur never saw the slash. But he felt it.

To the Maple Leaf Garden spectators it came with devastating suddenness. One moment Lafleur was leading a wave of red-jerseyed Canadiens to the attack; the next he was flinging his stick away and clutching his right hand in pain. There was no call from referee Art Skov.

After the game, a 2–2 tie, the Canadiens learned that Lafleur had suffered a broken knuckle and would be lost to the team for two or three weeks.

"Of course it was a slash," coach Scotty Bowman reflected after Lafleur had returned to the team. "But what difference would a penalty have made? Compared to losing Lafleur for a few weeks, the fact that Sittler didn't get a penalty is almost incidental."

Bowman could afford to be philosophical. The Canadiens had won seven of the nine games Lafleur missed, and were at last beginning to solidify their lead over the

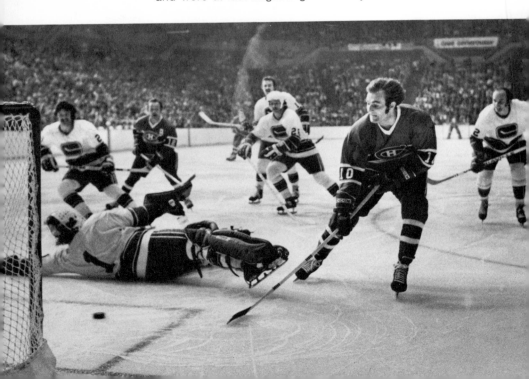

Los Angeles Kings, their closest pursuers for first place in the Norris Division of the Wales Conference. Lafleur himself had returned seemingly better than ever, with two goals and two assists against Washington. The star right wing was at last fulfilling the tremendous expectations almost everybody had had for him since he graduated from Junior hockey with a 130-goal season in 1970–71. This year his 53 goals and 119 points would set National Hockey League records for a right wing. By season's end, the cause of the brief layoff in February appeared nothing more than a routine injury, similar to those all hockey players must cope with. But this one was different in at least one respect: it was caused by a foul.

"Wood on wood," Skov reported to Referee-in-Chief Scotty Morrison. "Sittler's stick hit Lafleur's stick before it hit his hand."

"Wood on wood?" asked Bowman incredulously. "I've never heard of that."

Morrison explained later, citing a "degree of violence" theory. "Let's say you have Dave Keon [5 feet 9 inches, 163 pounds] checking Ken Hodge [6 feet 2 inches, 216 pounds]. Keon lands a two-hander on Hodge's stick, but because Hodge is so big and strong, he just shrugs it off. There's no point in calling a slash because there's no damage done. But say Hodge lands the two-hander on Keon's stick. In that case he may knock the stick out of Keon's hands, but if you didn't call slashing on Keon, it isn't fair to call it on Hodge in the same situation just because he's stronger. So what we'll do is call slashing only if the man himself, not his stick, is hit by the two-hander.

"In the Lafleur case, Sittler's stick landed on Lafleur's stick first and only then rode up, hitting Lafleur on the hand."

Nonsense, the Canadiens retorted. Tape marks from the stick were found on Lafleur's glove, they contended, and besides, the only way Lafleur's knuckle could have been broken was if Sittler's stick had struck it directly.

According to the rule book, the question of where Sittler's stick landed should have been academic. "A minor or major penalty, at the discretion of the Referee, shall be imposed on any player who impedes or seeks to impede the progress of an opponent by 'slashing' with his stick." (Rule 77.) Indeed, it shouldn't have mattered whether Sittler's stick hit Lafleur at all. "Referees should

After being slashed by Toronto's Darryl Sittler, Guy Lafleur missed eight games with a broken knuckle. But when he returned, he was as explosive as ever. Here he tucks one in against Vancouver.

penalize as 'slashing' any player who swings at an opposing player (whether in or out of range) *without actually striking him.*'' (Emphasis added.) The rule book leaves it to the referee to decide only whether a player did swing his stick in an attempt to impede another man's progress. If he did, the official is not supposed to decide what the effect of the slash was. There is no mention of degrees of violence, of big players and little players, of harm to the slashed player or just harrassment of him. The "wood on wood" concept is more than just a lax interpretation of the rule; it is a complete rewriting of it.

Because the Canadiens hardly missed Lafleur, the

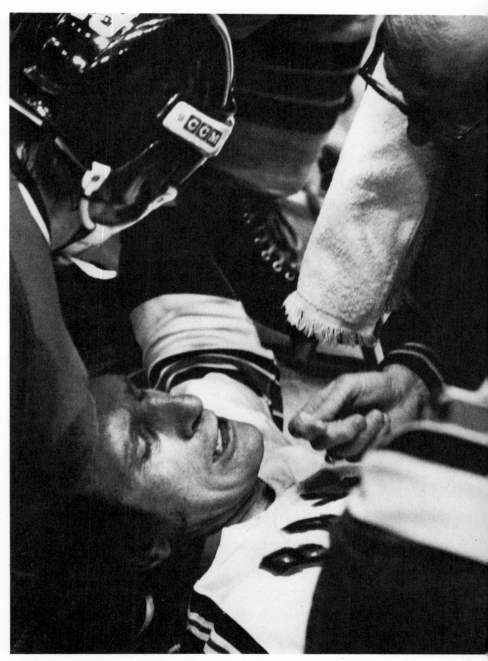

Hazards of the trade. *Opposite:* Mike Robitaille
displays stitches (note missing front teeth).
Above: Smelling salts are administered to Ranger
Dale Rolfe after he fractured his ankle.

pro hockey world could easily overlook the policy of foul-calling that indirectly led to his injury. Hockey players don't like to dwell on their injuries and certainly don't like to complain about them. Hockey is one of the world's most brutal team sports, and its players pride themselves on their ability to withstand punishment. They casually place their teeth in paper cups before a game or practice, and receive stitches without the luxury of a local anesthetic. They expect to play with injuries that would put other athletes on the sidelines or in a hospital.

Playing on a broken ankle, Bobby Baun of Toronto scored the winning goal in the sixth game of the 1964 Stanley Cup playoffs. While with the Chicago Black Hawks, Bobby Hull played one stretch of games with his jaw broken and wired together, though he was lean and weak from sipping his meals through a straw.

"I'll never forget my first game as team doctor for the Blues," recalls Dr. J. G. Probstein of St. Louis. "I was sitting down in the dressing room, listening to the game on the radio, when the door flies open and in tromps Noel Picard. He was one of our big defensemen, and he had a nasty cut over his eye that obviously needed stitches.

"Well, as I was scrubbing my hands, he got more impatient by the second. He kept telling me to hurry up, hurry up. Then, when I went to apply a local, he just shoved my hand away. 'Hurry up, Doc,' he said. 'Just sew it up.'

"So that's what I did—eleven stitches in that cut. No sooner did I cut the thread than he was on his feet. He grabbed his stick, started for the door, then suddenly turned around and said, 'Doc, how long you gonna be down here?'

" 'Till the end of the game,' I told him.

" 'Good,' he said, 'because the guy that did this to me will be down to see you in ten minutes.' "

Hockey players are famous for the grudges they hold, but they usually don't extend beyond the rink. In 1933, Toronto's Ace Bailey was fortunate to escape with his life after Eddie Shore knocked him to the ice with an illegal check from behind, causing Bailey to fracture his skull. Bailey's career was ended, but after he recovered, he cheerfully posed for pictures with Shore. Today, enemies on the ice may even be golfing companions or partners in a hockey school in the off-season. This is all part of hockey's code of understating the violence.

Were hockey the product of today's society, its players might be less willing to accept the dangers inherent in the game. However, from its formative years, hockey has borne the indelible stamp of the hard-working, hard-living, Canadian men who faced the hardships of the frontier with pride in their ability to endure punishment. "Hockey reflects us," remarked the late Lloyd Percival, a Canadian physical fitness expert. "In a game like hockey you have to have the emotional ability to keep going despite the knocks, without overreacting to the dangers."

Few players who have made it to the big league were well off when they were children. The rich kids usually gave up the earnest pursuit of hockey as too difficult, too demanding, and too dangerous. For those who made it to the big league, the game has traditionally been an escape from a life in a copper mine, a logging camp, or a paper mill. A few broken bones or missing teeth were a small price to pay.

"Hockey is so easy for the kids in the States today," says Jim Roberts, no bad guy but a veteran player for the Canadiens. "A kid gets cut, and maybe the only time his mother saw that much blood was when she had the kid. She gets hysterical. 'This game's too rough,' she

The bumps and bruises are not always the result of accidents. *Above left:* Polis cuffs Wilkins. *Above:* McKenzie skewers Barclay Plager.

says. 'My boy's going to get hurt bad, lose his teeth, and get cut up like all the rest of those hockey players.' She says, 'Either make this game so he doesn't get cut or he won't play.'

"Well, that's fine. The worst thing a parent can do is to force a kid to go out there and play hockey if he doesn't want to. Hockey is a rough game, a man's game. Getting cut once in a while, getting in an occasional fight, that's part of hockey."

Murray Oliver agrees. "The way I look at it, you expect to get hit and knocked around. That's all part of the game. So are the cheap shots you get now and then."

Hockey players understand and accept the violence, even as some spectators are appalled by it. "Take a forty-year-old American guy," says Bowman. "He's never played hockey and he sits up there in the stands and sees someone give someone else a two-hander. He can't believe grown men do this to one another, but hockey players understand it. They expect it. It's part of the knocks you take to make the NHL and then to stay here."

Bowman himself is a good example of one who has experienced the ugliest side of hockey violence and then more than forgiven his attacker. Bowman was a promising young Junior when he met defenseman Jean-Guy Talbot in a game at the Montreal Forum. A speedy forward, Bowman twice raced around Talbot for scores. On his third try Talbot brought his stick hammering down on Bowman's head, opening a gash that required 42 stitches to close. As they did with Green, doctors inserted a plate in Bowman's skull. They saved his life but not his career; at the age of 19, Bowman was finished as a hockey player.

Seventeen years later, in January, 1969, Bowman, as coach of the first-year St. Louis Blues, sat in his office, pondering ways to help his club in its struggle to make the playoffs. Suddenly, general manager Lynn Patrick came in with news that Talbot, by now an aging NHL veteran, had just been released by Detroit.

"Talbot's available," said Patrick.

"Can he still skate?" asked Bowman.

"Yeah."

Bowman never hesitated. "Then claim him."

With Talbot bolstering their back line, the Blues finished fourth and reached the finals in the Stanley Cup playoffs.

Stress injury: Dave Forbes twists his leg between the skates of Islander Dave Lewis and crumples on the leg of Lorne Henning.

Most incapacitating hockey injuries are not the result of fouls. They are "stress" injuries, often to the leg joints, that are inevitable in a game of hockey's speed and roughness. Skating at speeds up to 35 miles per hour, a player may easily strain his leg if he catches his skate in an imperfection in the ice or if he is body checked after having planted the leg. If the force of a collision is great enough, he may suffer a fracture. Whatever the leg injury, he is disabling a part of his body on which he must rest his weight. He can play with a welter of cuts and bruises but can't play on a knee or ankle that won't support him. Of the New York Rangers' 22 incapacitating injuries in 1974–75 (high in the NHL), there were nine strained or sprained knees, two broken legs, a broken foot, and a broken ankle. Only one man (Jean Ratelle) missed a game because of a cut.

Obviously, fouling is far from the prime cause of injury. But it is a contributor. Because injuries are so common, and because overcoming them is so much a player's ethic, the players themselves are not likely to protest.

But injuries are not always easy to overlook. Guy Lafleur was not the only victim. The Vancouver Canucks expected big things from Chris Oddleifson in 1974–75. The previous year they had given up their all-time single-season scoring leader, Bobby Schmautz, to acquire Oddleifson and Fred O'Donnell from the Boston Bruins. O'Donnell never reported to the Canucks (he jumped to the World Hockey Association), but Oddleifson alone

Keith Magnuson wore a covering for his hand when he fought with Canucks' Harold Snepsts, *above,* then with Chris Oddleifson, *opposite.* Oddleifson's jaw was broken, and he was forced to wear a specially designed helmet, *above right.*

seemed to make the deal worthwhile. He won an impressive five-year contract from the club before the start of the 1974–75 season.

Some two months into the season, the 25-year-old center was on his way to his best year as a pro. Finally given a chance to play regularly in the NHL, he responded with 27 points in 28 games. Led by goaltender Gary Smith and Oddleifson, the Canucks raced to the top of the Smythe Division in the Campbell Conference with 43 points in 31 games, 14 ahead of second-place St. Louis and 16 ahead of preseason-favorite Chicago. The year before, Vancouver had finished with 59 points in 78 games, third worst in the league.

The bubble burst on December 15 in Chicago. It was a game the floundering Black Hawks felt they had to win if they were to catch Vancouver, and they literally came out fighting. Barely a minute after the game began, Darcy Rota tangled with the Canucks' Gerry O'Flaherty, and Chicago's Ivan Boldirev engaged Gary Monahan. Referee Bruce Hood sent all four to the penalty box, but the mayhem continued. At 3:09, Vancouver rookie defenseman Harold Snepsts punished the Hawks' prime policeman, Keith Magnuson, in another fight. ("I wish they'd let me have another few minutes with that guy," Snepsts

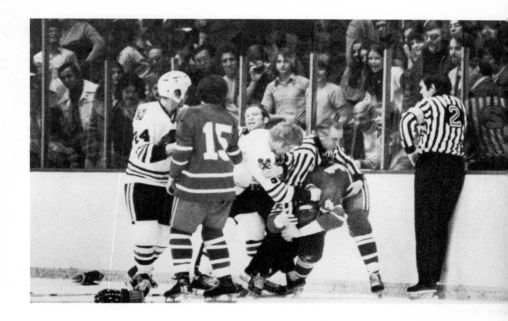

was reported to have said after the game.) Again Hood penalized the combatants, but when Magnuson returned to the game, he was not yet ready to play hockey. Apparently smarting from his defeat by Snepsts, Magnuson went heavily into the boards with Oddleifson. The two jostled briefly, then Magnuson shed his stick and gloves and began punching.

This time Magnuson won with a near knockout. Before the linesmen intervened, a hard right broke Oddleifson's jaw, leaving him bleeding and bent over in pain. After Magnuson was ushered to the penalty box (and Oddleifson to the dressing room), the officials noticed a peculiarity in the Chicago player's equipment. To protect a recently injured right wrist, Magnuson was wearing a hard plastic cover that extended from his forearm to slightly below the knuckles of his hand. At this point referee Hood banished Magnuson with a match penalty, invoking a new NHL rule that states, ". . . any player wearing tape or other material on his hands who cuts or injures an opponent during an altercation shall receive a match penalty." Magnuson was also fined $200, and Chicago had to play one man short for ten minutes, whereas the Canucks played shorthanded for only five (Oddleifson received a five-minute major for fighting).

Was it the plastic cover that broke Oddleifson's jaw? The Canucks said yes, Magnuson said no, and Clarence Campbell said he couldn't be sure—but it was beside the point. "The point is he, Magnuson, was wearing illegal equipment, and that's why the rule was passed," Campbell said. (The equipment was not illegal, but Campbell apparently meant that it, in effect, became illegal when used during the altercation.) A few days later, Campbell suspended Magnuson for three games.

Meanwhile, Oddleifson lay in a Chicago hospital undergoing surgery for a double fracture. The doctors estimated that he would be lost to the club for at least three to four weeks. He was gone for five and a half. Limited to a liquid diet, he lost 14 pounds in the first month of his convalescence. It was the third time in his career he had suffered a broken jaw.

The Canucks sorely missed him. A few days after his injury, they began their toughest stretch of the season— 9 of 12 games on the road. (The three home games were against top teams—Montreal, Boston, and Philadelphia.) Vancouver lost 10 of the 12 games (including 9 in a row), and when Oddleifson returned in late January, the 16-point lead over Chicago had shrunk to 2. To be sure, the Canucks were hurt by injuries to other players as well. They were already without defensemen John Grisdale and Mike Robitaille and forwards Dennis Vervegaert and Bobby Lalonde when they lost Oddleifson. But the loss of Oddleifson was the heaviest blow. Vancouver sports columnist Jim Taylor called him the best forward and one of the two key players on the team. (The other was goalie Gary Smith.)

When he finally did return, after missing 18 games, Oddleifson was still weak from loss of weight. He was further hindered by the football-type helmet he was forced to wear to protect his jaw. Made with bars across the mouth, the helmet obstructed his vision when he looked down, as a center often must, particularly on faceoffs. (Oddleifson is one of the better faceoff men in the league.)

His problems, and the team's, were not over. On March 16, in Oddleifson's first game in Chicago since the injury, Darcy Rota landed an elbow under Oddleifson's chin, thereby avoiding the bars in front of the mouth and bruising the still tender jaw. That shot cost Oddleifson three games but Rota nothing. Referee Art Skov called no penalty.

When the beleaguered center returned to action again, he was wearing a helmet with bars under the jaw as well as in front of it. These bars were lined on the inside with foam rubber padding. Now the helmet hampered both his vision and his breathing, because the foam rubber restricted the ventilation around his mouth.

Oddleifson finished the season with 16 goals and 35 assists, for 51 points. Had he played a full season at the pace he had set before the injury, he would have finished with 76 points. The Canucks finished in first place, but in the 49 games after Oddleifson's injury they scored only 43 points, the same number they had accumulated before the injury in only 31 games.

Like Lafleur, Oddleifson was initially more a victim of circumstance than of an aggressor's attempt to injure. Magnuson was wearing the plastic shield when he fought with Snepsts. "Why didn't they say anything on my first fight, which I lost?" he asked later. Probably, the officials didn't notice the cover, though Vancouver coach Phil Maloney said he tried to "get [referee Bruce] Hood's attention." However, even if the cover had been noticed, Hood was powerless to penalize Magnuson for it. The rule states that a player wearing such equipment is to be penalized with a match penalty only if he "cuts or injures an opponent during an altercation," and Magnuson did not harm Snepsts. Only after he hurt Oddleifson was he liable to a match penalty.

The Rota incident was another case of a missed foul. Play-by-play man Jim Robson of the Canucks called it "an obvious, intentional elbow missed by the referee."

Players in all sports are known to lean a little harder on those who are just returning after an injury. In hockey, where the unpenalized fouling is worse to start with, such extra "aggressiveness" is bound to have nasty consequences.

Rick Middleton of the Rangers was a leading contender for rookie of the year before Dennis Hextall of Minnesota "gave him the rub" in a game at Minnesota on January 15, 1975. The rookie had already missed six games with a sprained left knee. On January 5, Middleton suffered a cut lip that required 16 stitches, but with the aid of a football-type helmet to protect the injured area, he remained in the lineup. Despite the two injuries, he had 31 points in 33 games going into the game with the North Stars on the fifteenth—the first game that he played without the helmet.

Nine minutes into the first period, Middleton, Hextall, and a few other players piled into the sideboards in the Minnesota end, freezing the puck. The whistle blew and the players were starting to disengage when Hextall gratuitously poked his glove into Middleton's mouth. It was not a hard hit, but it caught the rookie off balance. As he fell backward, his left leg caught in the pileup. Middleton missed 24 games with a broken leg and finished the season with a lackluster total of 40 points in 47 games. (The top rookie scorer was Pittsburgh's Pierre Larouche, with 68 points.)

If Middleton was the Rangers' rookie sensation in 1974–75, Brad Park was the steadiest of their veterans. Though only 26, he had been a star almost from the moment he arrived in New York, in 1968–69, and the Rangers had come to depend on him. Severe injuries to defensemen Dale Rolfe and Ron Harris early in the year made it even more important that the Rangers' captain stay healthy. He lasted until 52 seconds into the second period on February 16, in a game at Madison Square Garden, when rambunctious Toronto rookie Dave ("Tiger") Williams took his second run at Rangers goalie Gilles Villemure.

Midway through the first period Williams had blind-sided Villemure, knocking him to the ice. Because Villemure was not the last man to play the puck, the check

was illegal, but it provoked no immediate retaliation from the Rangers or call from referee Wally Harris. Park was not on the ice then, but he was when Williams tried a similar maneuver at the start of the second period. This time the rookie hit Villemure somewhat less heavily, as the goalie strayed from his crease. Park retaliated anyway. He charged at Williams and slammed him from behind into the boards behind the net. Referee Harris called Park for a two-minute roughing penalty, but the Rangers' star never made it to the penalty box. When Park rebounded off the check and came down, the ice gave way beneath his left skate, the skate stuck in the crevice, and "something snapped" in the defenseman's left knee. The injury, officially called a strained left knee, cost Park 15 games. Before he was injured, the Rangers were 21–12–8. While he was gone, the team was only 5–8–2.

In New York no one seemed to notice that the injury to Park was precipitated by fouling—first by Williams' two provocations, then by Park's retaliation. The New York *Times* reported that Park's check was "a retaliation play which drew a thundering roar of applause from Garden spectators." News of the injury caused a furor over the ice condition at the Garden—widely denounced, even by some Rangers themselves, as having the worst ice in the league. There was no editorial comment in sports columns or in the stands about the game conditions under which the injury occurred. After all, hockey players go slamming into and bouncing off the boards on clean plays as well as on fouls, and in either case they need to have a well-kept ice surface on which to land. It was just a coincidence that Park happened to be injured on a fouling play.

It was also a coincidence that he was injured at all. Bad as the Garden ice may have been, it was coincidental that Park's skate lodged in an imperfection in it. It was an unhappy coincidence too that Sittler's stick happened to break Lafleur's knuckle, that Magnuson happened to land a blow on Oddleifson's jaw, that Hextall's rub happened to catch Middleton off balance. Hundreds of players are slashed each year without being injured; dozens fight with Magnuson without getting their jaws broken; scores are rubbed by Hextall without breaking their legs. Though some are more freakish than others, most injuries from fouling, like all other injuries, can be blamed on bad luck.

The 1974–75 Rangers lost captain and star defenseman Brad Park, *opposite left and right,* when he charged Toronto's Dave Williams. In the weeks Park was missing, the Rangers plummeted.

Nevertheless, Park would not have been hurt had he not felt it necessary to take an illegal run at Williams. If players take enough full-speed runs into the boards, legal or illegal, sooner or later they are going to get hurt.

Park charged Williams because of an unwritten rule among hockey players that the goalie should not be body checked. In this day of roaming goalies, the temptation is ever present for an aggressive forward to check a goalie whose efforts outside the crease may be at least as important as those of any forward or defenseman in clearing the puck from the defensive zone. Thus, referees do not call checks against goalies any more tightly than those against other players. Unfortunately, most players don't accept this policy. For the most part, they leave goalies unchecked and get riled when an opponent violates the code. Fouling is the players' way of resolving the discrepancy between how the referees treat the goalies and how the players think the goalies should be treated.

On January 18, 1975, Los Angeles defenseman Bob Murdoch suffered a badly battered nose in a fight with the Canadiens' Doug Risebrough in the first period of a game in Montreal. Murdoch left the game for repairs, and returned in the third period just in time to see Montreal's Serge Savard knock down Kings goalie Rogatien Vachon, who had left his crease to clear a loose puck.

Murdoch did not hesitate. He immediately charged Savard and wrestled him to the ice. Although neither player threw any damaging blows, Murdoch again injured his nose in the scuffle. "Nobody knocks down our goaltender," Murdoch declared afterward. "Savard better watch out. The next time he does it, I'll bleed all over him again."

Although the effects vary and are difficult to assess, injuries make a difference to both players and teams. To an individual player an injury can mean a lost award, a missed bonus, decreased long-range earning power, even a lost job. While he is sidelined, an injured player may make the mistake of fretting over such things. It makes him temperamental, even reclusive. But it does keep him occupied—suddenly finding himself without the strenuous physical activity that was the central part of his life, he may feel he has nothing else to do but to worry.

When he does return, his first instinct is to make up for his layoff by overworking himself in practice. If he does, he risks reinjury. But no matter how intelligently or industriously he practices, he won't regain his peak condition until he experiences the grueling regimen of regular competition. Then he faces another psychological barrier.

"I've seen hundreds of guys get hurt, some bad, some not so bad," says Buffalo general manager Punch Imlach. "And in my experience I'd have to say that when someone has been hurt pretty bad, you find him holding back out there when he comes back. He's not afraid. He wouldn't be out there if he was. But somehow he's just not as aggressive as he was before he was hurt. He won't admit it. If his record shows that he's not up to par, he'll just say he came back too soon. It's probably psychological, something subconscious holding him back. But in this game, if you're going to play and try not to get injured, you're not worth ten cents."

To a team, injuries vary from blessings in disguise to undisguised disasters. Montreal barely missed Lafleur for nine games but already-ailing Vancouver was deeply wounded when it lost Oddleifson. The loss of Gilbert Perreault doomed Buffalo's chances at a playoff spot in 1973–74, but when the Sabres lost him in 1974–75, Jim Lorentz substituted ably and the club never faltered.

If a team is thin on reserves and in a precarious position in the standings, the pressure on the front office to trade a promising but not yet mature youngster for an experienced stopgap can become intense. The risk is obvious: by trading youth for experience, a team jeopardizes its future.

"Our policy has always been to put the strongest club on the ice without sacrificing our future," says Sam Pollock, general manager of the Montreal Canadiens. "Maybe if a club hasn't won for a long time, they might want to pick up a veteran in exchange for a draft choice. I'm not saying everyone should play it the way we do. But this team will never, ever, mortgage its future for short-term gain."

Montreal is an exception. Always well stocked with talent, the Canadiens are usually capable of playing over injuries that would stagger most other clubs. Indeed, when a member of the Canadiens is lost, it can provide the only break one of their talented youngsters needs. "After Henri Richard broke his ankle in the twelfth game

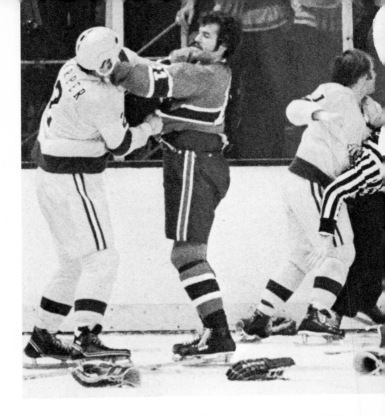

of the season, on a Saturday night at the Forum, we were six, four, and two," recalls coach Bowman. "We met after the game and Pollock decided to bring up Doug Risebrough as a replacement at center. That was fine with me; the kid had had a good training camp. But I wanted to bring up Mario Tremblay too. We'd had some other problems on the club, and I felt the presence of a couple of hungry kids might make a difference. Besides, bringing them both up at the same time would mean less pressure on each of them. Well, we went into Boston Garden that Sunday night and beat the Bruins four-one. We've been a different team ever since. And believe me, those two kids have had an awful lot to do with it."

More common is the case of the Chicago Black Hawks, one of the league's most heavily injured clubs in 1974–75. The Hawks finished a disappointing third in the Smythe Division. General manager Tommy Ivan says, "Where injuries really hurt you is in the key games— games in which you can beat someone you've got to beat, or a game in which you have an opportunity to shove a contender further behind you in the standings. I'm not using our injuries this year as an alibi. There's no

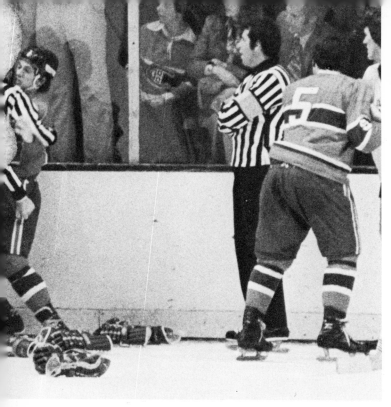

Montreal's newest pepper pot, Doug Risebrough (helmeted at center), got his chance when the aging Henri Richard was injured. Risebrough has been part of Canadiens' battle plan ever since.

excuse for playing below your capabilities, but in those key games, yeah, I'd have to say that's when you really miss key players who are out with injuries."

Fouling can cause injuries, and injuries hurt the players and the clubs. But there is a more direct cost of fouling—it can hurt the style and caliber of play itself. Good hockey is a game of constant movement. The best hockey adds crunching body contact, precise passing, artful stickhandling, and furious skating. But all these elements are predicated on the game flowing. When the linesmen are constantly whistling down infractions and the referee is forever assessing penalties, hockey cannot be vibrant. The whistles, however necessary to maintain order, stop the flow.

Obviously, the best games are the ones that regulate themselves, striking on their own the delicate balance between order and energy. The players play within the rules without being hampered by them, and the officials melt into the background.

Unfortunately, this doesn't just happen. First, it takes highly motivated players—not always common in this postexpansion era of easy money and relatively great

job security. Ten years ago there were roughly 120 players in major league hockey, the only level at which a man
could earn even a modest wage playing the game. The
rules were simple and brutal. To keep his job, a player
had to follow orders and avoid injuries. If he stepped out
of line or faltered, he was gone. The results were vicious
competition and fairly skilled, disciplined, and spirited
play.

"Before expansion, there were only six goaltenders
in the NHL, and they played sixty-five or seventy games a
year," recalls Gump Worsley, who played for the New
York Rangers, Montreal Canadiens, and Minnesota North
Stars. "We not only had the pressure of the job itself,
but the pressure of not doing badly for too long. There
were ten or fifteen other goaltenders around, waiting to
take our jobs. *That* was pressure."

Management never failed to remind the players how
fortunate they were to be in the NHL. Detroit general
manager Jack Adams carried a stack of train tickets
everywhere he went, lest any Red Wing somehow enter-
tain the idea that he was indispensable.

Pat Quinn, now a veteran defenseman with the
Atlanta Flames, remembers, "Before expansion I was
with Toronto, and Punch Imlach would walk into our
dressing room before a game and wave a plane ticket
to Pittsburgh under our nose. He'd already have it made
out, in your name. *That* was intimidation, and intimidation
of the worst kind. The threat of being sent down, not
knowing if you'd ever be back again—that in itself made
an awful lot of chickens courageous."

With thousands of players in Junior hockey working
toward their dream of making the NHL, and hundreds in
the minors almost there, there was not only intense
pressure but a special sense of pride and accomplish-
ment that spurred the players to produce their best.
Occupying one of the 120 spots in the NHL was indeed
an honor; to do so meant that one had risen to the
top of the most widely followed and prestigious profes-
sion in Canada. Even if a player departed soon after
making the big league, he had no cause for shame; all of
Canada knew that only the unusually gifted lasted for
more than a few years.

"When I first came up with the Red Wings I saved
every newspaper article that mentioned my name," recalls Gordie Howe, "not because I had a big ego, 'cause
I didn't. It was because I expected to last only a year or

two, and later on, if anyone asked, I wanted to be able to prove that I had played in the National Hockey League.''

Today, Howe is a millionaire, having parlayed his fame into fortune by joining the Houston Aeros of the World Hockey Association. He well remembers that when he was a blossoming star with the Red Wings he was not especially well paid. "Every summer my neighbor would hitch a trailer to his car and take off on a two-week vacation," Howe recalls. "But I couldn't afford it. Here I was, Gordie Howe, and I had to hold down a summer job to make ends meet."

Today there are more than 600 players in big league hockey. The average salary of an NHL pro has risen some tenfold in ten years, to $70,000. In the disconcertingly literal parlance of the game, today's major leaguers are not as "hungry."

"Today you almost have to *ask* a player to get off his ass," says Kansas City general manager Sid Abel. "You can't tell him to do it or threaten him into it. If he's got any ability, he knows there's probably a job for him somewhere else.

"And you know, it's not his fault. It's just human nature. When someone feels secure he tends to lose that hungry, competitive edge. When he's not really worried about his future, it's only natural for him to take the path of least resistance."

On the other hand, expansion and the tremendous financial pressures on a club's management to produce a winner have opened up the game to talented players who never had a chance before. No longer do potential stars languish in the farm systems of the top teams while the have-not clubs muddle for a decade with a succession of third-rate players. Expansion diluted the talent pool, but it also showed it to be deeper than people had thought. With drafting reforms, the talent has been more equitably distributed. The result is far from a drop in the level of play. The dynasties of the Montreal Canadiens and the Detroit Red Wings are, more than likely, things of the past. Yet the infant Buffalo Sabres, New York Islanders, Atlanta Flames, and Vancouver Canucks put the well-established Black Hawks, Bruins, and Rangers of the fifties to shame.

Buffalo's Punch Imlach favorably compares his young Sabres to his Stanley Cup champion Maple Leafs of the sixties. And Claude Ruel, the former Montreal coach who is now the club's director of player personnel, says that the Canadiens' current defense of Guy Lapointe, Serge Savard, Don Awrey, and Larry Robinson is the most formidable in the team's history. "There is no Doug Harvey out there," he says. "But no other group can touch all four of them together."

The players of today are generally faster, bigger, stronger, and better than their counterparts of a decade ago. They are more intelligent and better balanced emotionally—in short, less crazy. Realizing how much money they are worth, they are more reluctant to indulge in the stick-swinging lunacy of years ago, or to jeopardize in any other way their lucrative careers. "Hockey players are making a lot more money today, and as a result they expect more and better treatment," says the trainer of the St. Louis Blues, Tommy Woodcock. "If they think there's something seriously wrong with them, they want to know what you're going to do before you do it. You can't just say 'Get in the whirlpool.' They want you to explain to them what's wrong and what you plan to do about it."

If there has been an overall decline in the quality of play since expansion and the dramatic rise in salaries, it cannot be attributed only to dilution of talent and complacency bred of easy money. Athletes can be motivated by considerations other than money and fear of losing their jobs. If this were not true, there would be no championship-caliber teams today in any of the major sports, all of which reward their players generously, even exorbitantly, whether they win or lose.

Obviously, not all athletes today lose their competitive edge because they are well paid. Even hockey players of marginal skills, who are sometimes accused more than the stars of being overpaid and underworked, can produce fine hockey, as players like Bob Kelly, Terry Harper, J. P. Parise, and Ron Schock prove. If pro hockey is not as vibrant as it could be, the reason is not simply complacent players.

Clearly, a fine hockey game requires more than skilled and motivated players. The Russia-Team Canada series proved that. The finest hockey players in the world could, and should, have produced the world's finest hockey. Often they did, but too often the play suffered from fouling. In the most infamous instance of excessive fouling, Bobby Clarke slashed the ankle of Russian star Valery Kharlamov, sidelining him for much of the sixth and all of the seventh game (both won by Team Canada)

of the eight-game series. "It suddenly hit me that Khar-lamov was the guy who was killing us while I was only holding my own," Clarke recalls. "I realized immediately that someone had to do something about him. It's not something I was really proud of, but I honestly can't say I was ashamed to do it."

Excessive violence and fouling can, and frequently do, injure the game itself. That ideal balance between order and energy is elusive in hockey; indeed, there are many games that seem to lack both. The players skate listlessly and formlessly, until the discriminating spectator leaves the arena feeling he has just escaped from a sluggishly pitching ship. Bad hockey can make you queasy. In such cases a shot of violence may be a healthy tonic. Red Fisher, the veteran Montreal hockey writer, notes, "I've seen some dull hockey games that fighting made more interesting." But he acknowledges that the opposite is equally true: "There have been some good hockey games ruined by fighting."

When there is no energy in a game, violent fouling

Bobby Clarke moves to aid fellow Team Canada member Yvan Cournoyer in his battle with Soviet Valery Vasiliev. Clarke aided the Canadiens as much with hatchet work as with his hockey skill.

provides some. It may shake the players from their lethargy into disciplined as well as aggressive play. But when the game is already disciplined and aggressive, violent fouling gets in the way. The crowd howls with pleasure over the headhunting, but if the game is already a good one, the pyrotechnics are no bonus. They sap the game of its energy as well as its order. Inevitably the play stops, sticks and gloves litter the ice, and the combatants indulge in the great ritual of bombastic threat and counterthreat. Eventually, the litter is collected, the penalties assessed, and the combatants safely ensconced in the penalty box. It may have been a fine spectacle, but the tempo of the game has been interrupted and perhaps lost. When play resumes, it is apt to be ragged, for the players are winded, disorganized,

Fighting and fouling break up the flow of the game and dull the luster of the stars. *Above:* The aftermath—Leafs and Sabres catch their breath after brawling. *Opposite:* Orr escapes a hook.

and off their timing. Perhaps the penalties broke up a line that had been working well together. In any case, the game has stopped and lost its flow. In more ways than one, a fight is a hard act to follow.

On April 3, 1975, the Rangers and Flyers engaged in one of their many battles. It could have been a great game. The Rangers badly needed to win to regain second place from the upstart Islanders. The Flyers needed the two points in their quest for most points in the league. But instead of using their energies and talents to play hockey, the teams spent the first period and a half fighting. It was a grand spectacle and nobody got hurt. The only damage was to the game. By the third period, the teams were too tired to fight or to play hockey, so they did neither. It was a close game (a 1–1 tie), but except for sporadic bursts, it was not well played. The fans went home having seen 30 minutes of first-class hockey brawling and 60 minutes of subpar hockey.   •

Even if it doesn't cause injuries or erupt into fisticuffs, excessive fouling can deprive hockey of showcase skills. When Guy Lafleur or Gilbert Perreault cannot skate freely because a defender is hacking away at his ankles

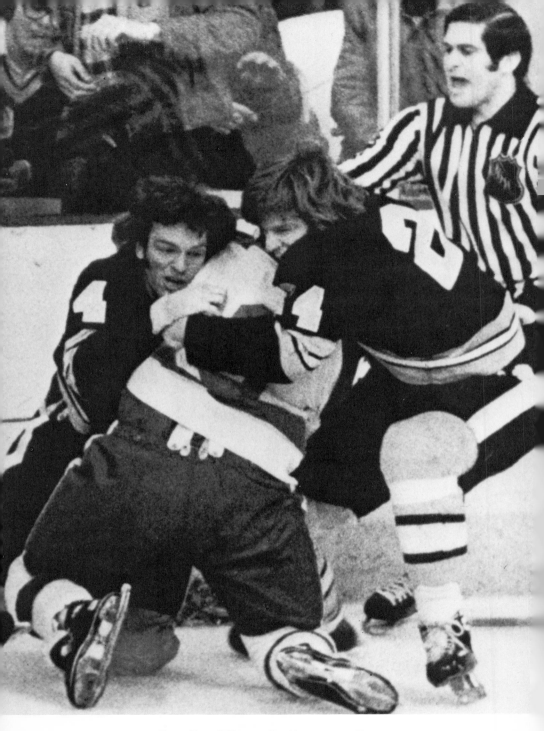

Above: Dave Forbes, assisted by teammate Terry
O'Reilly, tangles with North Star Henry Boucha
in the fight that preceded the one in which Forbes
nearly poked out Boucha's eye. *Opposite:* Forbes
in civvies after indictment and suspension.

or elbowing him in the face along the boards, he is suffering more than the harrassment of extra tight checking, which every star deserves and expects. These are cheap shots, to which the talented victim has only the most limited choice of responses. If he retaliates, he fulfills the objectives of the hacker by being sent to the penalty box; if he accepts the punishment, the game deteriorates to its lowest level, a fouling contest. In either case the level of play declines and the old hockey maxim is proved again: "If you can't beat 'em in the alley, you can't beat 'em in the rink."

At its best, fouling encourages players to overcome the abuse so that they can use their hockey skills. If they succeed, the game is as good as it was before; if not, the game suffers.

Today, though the game is faster than ever before, the skills of stick handling and even passing are often neglected. Most teams are content to carry the puck to center ice, dump it into the offensive zone, and try to knock the retrieving team off it. It is a physically demanding game, but not altogether an exciting one. In effect, the "dump it in" pattern cuts the rink in half, all but negating the greater speed of today's skaters. It allows little continuity to the play because the puck is often left uncontrolled. This style is so simple and repetitive that it quickly becomes boring.

When fouling proliferates, it encourages this crude hockey. Great hockey requires tight, physical checking to give shape to its sophisticated skating, stick handling, and passing. Fouling can wreck the skills and the exciting pattern they create. After solid checking has weeded out the loose play, fouling is a pestilence that kills quality.

There is another cost of excessive violence, so rare

that its implications are not yet clear. It demands examination, because it has already proved to be a greater liability to the game than all the others combined, and the effect may well become worse. That is the cost of career-debilitating injury from excessive violence, and the threat of outside regulation that such incidents provoke.

Pro hockey has for a long time more or less accepted the particularly ugly results of excessive violence as a rare if traumatic part of the game. Because players are more sensible today, such incidents are less frequent than they used to be, but the threat of outside intervention when they do occur is probably greater now, as the unhappy experience of Dave Forbes and Henry Boucha proved. That much-publicized incident occurred on January 4, 1975, in a game at Minnesota. Early in the first period, the North Stars' Boucha went after a puck along the boards, followed by the Bruins' Forbes. Elbows flew and sticks clanged against the glass, and in the ensuing fight Boucha won a clear-cut decision over Forbes. Referee Ron Wicks gave both men two-minute roughing minors and five-minute fighting majors.

Emotions carried over into the penalty box, where the two players exchanged verbal threats and Forbes reportedly told Boucha that he would shove his stick down his throat.

When the penalties expired, Boucha began skating toward the Minnesota bench on the opposite side of the ice. Forbes, skating behind Boucha and to his right, reportedly said, "Okay, let's go now," and with that he swung at Boucha, the butt end of his stick striking Boucha in the right eye. The Minnesota player fell to the ice, his hands covering his face. As Boucha lay in what reports described as "an ever-widening pool of blood," Forbes pounced on him and continued to throw punches until Murray Oliver of the North Stars pulled him away.

Boucha was carried from the ice on a stretcher and rushed to a nearby hospital, where 25 stitches were required to close the cut beside his right eye. Still more were needed inside the eyelid. When an eye patch was removed five days later, Boucha complained of double vision. New X rays revealed a small fracture at the floor of the right eye socket. An eye specialist performed remedial surgery the next day. Boucha missed 19 games, but when he returned, he was still hampered by poor vision because his eye did not move properly in its socket.

After spending more than eight hours with the involved parties, NHL President Campbell suspended Forbes for ten games. A Hennepin County (Minnesota) grand jury had already begun to investigate the incident, and on January 17, Forbes was indicted for aggravated assault with a dangerous weapon. The action made Forbes the first professional athlete in the United States ever to be brought before a judge by civil authorities for an act committed during competition. The trial ended in a hung jury and Forbes went free, but the issue remained unresolved. Pro hockey hadn't been acquitted.

"Are we supposed to sit here and say, 'Boys will be boys?'" asked Hennepin County Attorney Gary Flakne, who announced the indictment. "I agree that hockey is a contact sport, but there seems to be a line, which the grand jury found and I agree with, beyond which something other than good-natured hard contact becomes assault."

The specter of hockey being in effect taken to court is not a pleasant one even for those who believe that more needs to be done to control the excessive violence in the game. If a trial jury upholds a grand jury's distinction between part-of-the-game violence and criminal assault, it would seem to open the door to civil suits as well as criminal indictments. It would then quickly become apparent that a hockey game is not best refereed in a courtroom.

"If this civil intervention is pursued to trial," said Campbell, a lawyer himself, "we will have to give great thought to the future of our game. As far as I am concerned, civil authority is not equipped to deal with this type of situation."

Nevertheless, as Campbell himself admitted, "Something must be done to control the violence in our game. I hear ten discipline cases each week. And over the course of a season, I suspect I hear at least ten cases where the civil authorities might think that a crime was committed."

Because hockey has failed to regulate itself, civil authorities have felt the need to step in. Other sports have taken the necessary steps to control, if not eliminate, excessive violence. Hockey has not. With the threat of outside intervention, the incentive to reform may now become an ultimatum—clean up the game or else.

3.
The Sell,
the Strategy, and
the System

Everybody in the United States has grown up playing basketball, baseball, or football, but almost everybody who goes to a hockey game in this country has never been on the ice. It baffles me.

Billy Cunningham
Forward for the Philadelphia 76ers
of the National Basketball Association

Less than a decade ago, major league hockey consisted of six teams that collectively called themselves the National Hockey League. After almost fifty years of operation, the NHL had developed a rich tradition and a devoted following, but, in the United States at least, the league's appeal was limited to the four NHL cities—Boston, Chicago, Detroit, and New York. For all any sports fan in Los Angeles or Atlanta knew or cared, a hat trick was magician's mischief, Toe Blake an obscure field-goal kicker, Rocket Richard and Boom Boom Geoffrion a French-Canadian tag team act, and Alex Delvecchio a comer in the Detroit Mafia.

The NHL owners suffered such misconceptions about their product with little regret. Gratifying as it would have been to have Americans, as well as Canadians, embrace hockey nationwide, the owners saw no compelling reason to solicit new members for their cozy club. The NHL had never numbered more than ten teams, and the same six had comprised it since 1942, when the old Brooklyn Americans folded. Twelve years later, when the Chicago Black Hawks were floundering in deep financial trouble, it was the owner of the Detroit Red Wings, James Norris, Jr., who came to the rescue. (Norris also owned a piece of Madison Square Garden and of Boston Garden, and had loaned money to the Canadiens.) When Norris left the Red Wings in the hands of his son, Bruce, and daughter, Marguerite, it was said that NHL really stood for "Norris House League."

Of course, any elite clan of millionaires will have its squabbles, and this one was no exception, but the owners' two common interests—hockey and making money—made their close partnership worthwhile. When the Chicago Black Hawks started selling out Chicago Stadium in the late 1950s, the league as a whole was playing to 96 percent of capacity. All the owners were making money—and (therefore) having fun. No matter that professional baseball and football were expanding into

One needn't have played hockey to enjoy watching
it. Indeed, hockey fans usually gain
most of their hockey exercise in the stands.

other cities; hockey saw no reason to embark on any such sweeping changes.

Then two factors dramatically increased the size and scope of pro hockey almost overnight. First, the owners realized they had an opportunity to reap a golden harvest through a national television contract, provided the league expanded into a nationwide circuit. While pondering that happy possibility, the executives were given another, more ominous incentive to expand. The success of the NHL had not gone unnoticed, and rumors were circulating that a rival league might try to claim a piece of the profits of big league hockey. The game was going to expand, and the NHL had little choice but to lead the gold rush itself, before somebody else did.

In June, 1966, NHL President Clarence Campbell called a press conference in Montreal to announce that the NHL had decided to double in size, an expansion of unprecedented proportions in big league sports. Eighteen months later, the six new franchises, including two on the West Coast, began to operate in a newly created division of the NHL. Over the next few years, six more teams were added, bringing the NHL to a sprawling eighteen-team syndicate. Undaunted, a new league, the World Hockey Association, began in 1972, and with its twelve teams swelled the total number of big league hockey cities to more than two dozen.

Across North America, pro hockey commands a legion of followers more knowledgeable, more diverse, and more numerous than ever before. In Boston, the traditional center of American hockey, raucous working men come to grimy old Boston Garden to marvel over hockey's golden boy, Bobby Orr, to salute the scoring feats of his swarthy companion, Phil Esposito, and to cheer the pugnacious Terry O'Reilly, one of the few rightful heirs of the big bad Bruins of the sixties. In Houston, new hockey country, the crowds need no deep knowledge of the game to appreciate the extravagant production numbers of Gordie Howe & Sons. In Montreal the savants of the game have momentarily forgotten their grumbling over expansion to enjoy the blossoming of another fine Canadiens team and the blooming of its leader, Guy Lafleur, in "the Year of the Flower." In Los Angeles, the vastly improved Kings attract a talk-show slew of celebrities—Telly Savalas, Don Rickles, Karl Malden, Xavier Cugat, and Charo, among others. In St. Louis, the Blues draw hundreds of richly clothed and

The hockey crowd includes, *clockwise from opposite bottom,* the fashionable, the famous, the frantic, and the folksy.

coiffed women in Halston fashions and mink or sable, their male companions in three-hundred dollar double-knit designer suits, silk shirts, and star sapphire pinky rings.

Clearly, attending pro hockey games is by no means a lower-class diversion. In Toronto's Maple Leaf Gardens, the best seats for the season cost $12 each. In New York's Madison Square Garden, they are $10.50. In Philadelphia, a pair of rink-side seats for the season cost $798, not including 42 games' worth of cocktails and dinners in the Blueliners' Club, parking, and incidentals such as the playoffs, for which management adds an extra dollar or two to the price of each ticket. Even so, Philadelphia owner Ed Snider says he could sell a hundred thousand tickets to some Flyers games. "You wouldn't believe the names of some of the people I have to turn down, and I'm the *owner*," he laments. "But you can't sell what you don't have."

During the 1974–75 season, more than 10 million people, a record number, paid their way into arenas in the United States and Canada to watch NHL teams perform. In the WHA, the total was 3.3 million, up 47 percent from the year before.

In Canada, where hockey is a way of life from the frozen ponds of rural Flin Flon, Kirkland Lake, and Trois Rivières to the big league cities, the love of the game springs from a deep understanding of it. But in the United States, where thousands of fans have yet to fully grasp

More than their American counterparts, Canadian fans are supposed to appreciate the finer points of the game. But the fights in Toronto, *above,* and in Vancouver, *opposite,* are just as popular as the fights south of the border.

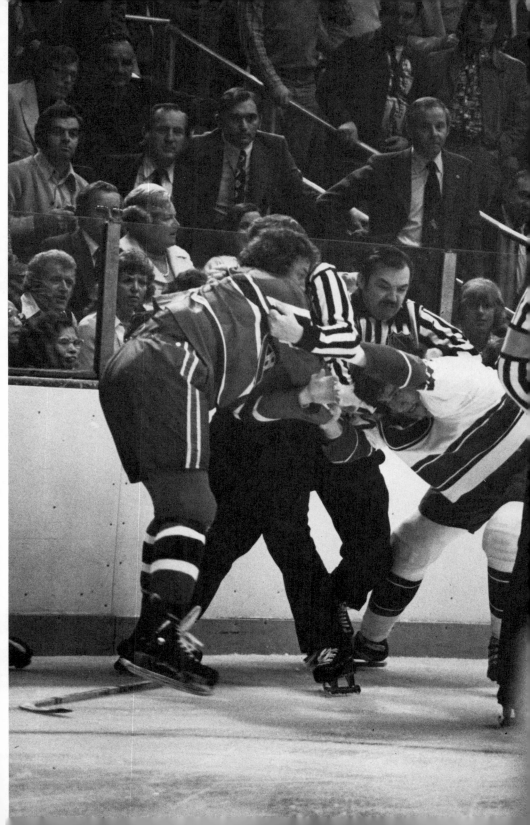

Greg Sheppard (19) and Bob Nevin are relative
lightweights in the fight game, yet
even they can stage an entertaining spectacle.

the rules of the game, let alone the frontiersman nature of those who play it for a living, its appeal is at least partly a novelty, an exciting difference for those who were weaned on conventional American sports. To these fans, pro hockey is more than the uncanny grace and violent collisions of ten hurtling bodies pursuing the deceptively simple task of guiding a rubber disk into a cage. It is also a spectacle of unabashed bare-knuckle brawling on skates.

"Southern people love stock-car racing and football, and in hockey I think they find a blend of both," says Atlanta general manager Cliff Fletcher, who has watched Dixie respond enthusiastically to a game it had barely

heard of five years ago. "Hockey has the speed of racing and the body contact of football. And the players are right there in front, where everyone can see. There's no question that they love the fights. If we have a fight one night, that's all people are talking about the next day."

When two players suddenly drop the gloves, many in the audience react as they would at no other sports event. Decorously dressed women, their carefully casual, streaked hair flying, leap to their feet and thump Hermes purses on the heads of patrons in front of them. Normally mild-mannered males, drawing courage from the rows of seats between themselves and the ice, shake their fists in anger and hurl beer cups, obscenities, even

Left: Los Angeles' Bob Murdoch entertains the home crowd by wrestling Bruins bad boy Wayne Cashman. *Above:* An exhilarating experience.

challenges at the players below. When the combatants eventually tumble to the ice in a panoply of pads, suspenders, and sweat-soaked undershirts, the cheers roll out of the stands in waves. "The fans love the fights; there's no doubt about that," Chicago's Keith Magnuson says flatly.

Charles Loudermilk, an Atlanta businessman who has invested in the Flames, may be speaking for more of America than the South when he says, "Southern people don't understand hockey yet, but they understand fights. We've done pretty well in three years. We've won a lot more than people predicted we would. But I'm convinced we could put another thousand people in The Omni for every game if we had a fighting team—which we don't."

"Minnesota is supposed to be pretty sophisticated hockey country," says the North Stars' Murray Oliver. "But if there's been a fight in a game that's all they're talking about the next day at the golf course."

In Philadelphia, fans show up at the Spectrum wearing World War I German combat helmets. Others produce signs such as "Lady Byng Died in Philadelphia."

Fans in the old-line hockey stronghold of Boston have always loved the ostentatious machismo types. Even in the fifties and early sixties, Boston's darkest years in the NHL, the fans flocked to Boston Garden to see such bad men as Fern Flaman, Leo Boivin, and Ted Green. Then, in the late sixties, they stormed the newsstands for a *Sports Illustrated* cover story entitled "Bobby Orr and the Animals."

In 1968, the St. Louis Blues sent a fan magazine to their season ticket holders with an article that began, "West of St. Louis, on Route 66, a billboard beckons sightseers to Meramec Caverns, 'The Hideout of the Notorious James Brothers, Missouri's Most Famous Badmen.'

"Most famous? Not any more. Move over Jesse and Frank. Make room for Barclay and Bob Plager, whose exploits in the National Hockey League bring forth anguished cries: 'The Plager brothers ride again.' "

Today, as always, the quickest way for a player to establish a demonstrative following is to earn his credentials as a fighter. Keith Magnuson of Chicago, Dennis Hextall of Minnesota, Terry O'Reilly of Boston, Battleship Bob Kelly of Pittsburgh, Terry Harper of Los Angeles, Garry Howatt of the Islanders, Bert Wilson of the Rangers, and of course, Dave Schultz (among others) of Philadelphia, all attracted notice first, and in most cases foremost, because of their fighting skills. The Islanders' publicist calculated, "I figure Garry [Howatt] had thirty fights, won twenty-eight, lost one and tied one, in 1973–74. The fans love him."

Thousands of fans around the league follow the fights and the fighters as closely as they do the standings. Indeed, the fighters are ranked in their own standings, however unofficially, informally, and unobjectively. Every hockey announcer and newspaperman learns the brawling capabilities of the players and passes them along to the fans, though usually not without local prejudice. The Black Hawks' Darcy Rota, a New York broadcaster has said, will not fight outside Chicago. The same announcer has alleged that the Flyers don't allow Bobby Clarke to fight his own battles. Gossip has it that Phil Esposito would rather complain to officials than fight his battles himself.

Clearly, fighting appeals to many people, though they may be reluctant to admit it, or even incapable of fully recognizing it. Competition is the basic attraction of almost all spectator sports, and fighting is competition in its rawest form. Hockey fans are far from the only sports fans who, once their competitive fires are raging, find it difficult to draw the line between competitive sport and brutal competition. Football fans do not go to their games expecting a Franco Harris and an Alan Page to shed their helmets and go at it, but the fans go wild if they do.

And why not? It is illogical to accept a perfectly legal blind-side tackle as part of the game and condemn fighting as a brutal excess. In both hockey and football, fighting is far less violent and dangerous than other aspects of the game.

A number of psychologists see in hockey and its brawling an opportunity for a fan to pour out his frustrations, act out his fantasies, loose his aggressions, and forget his problems. Hockey fans (and fans of other violent sports as well) are said to feel confused, stepped on, and impotent—children longing for simplicity in an age of complexity. In the rush to psychoanalyze, it has perhaps been overlooked that fighting contributes more to hockey than an opportunity for the fans to forget their woes. Like the opera, theater, or a classical music concert, the audience for each of which presumably includes some people acting out fantasies or otherwise escaping the problems of twentieth-century life, a hockey game with a fight can be a gripping experience.

Some very well-adjusted people have found the spectacle of pro hockey, fights and all, irresistible—the ebb and flow of end-to-end action, the brightly clad bodies charging up and down the ice, colliding, sprawling, and being slammed into the boards so hard that the building seems to shake. Add to this a menacing glare, an elbow or glove in the face, a retaliatory rap on the

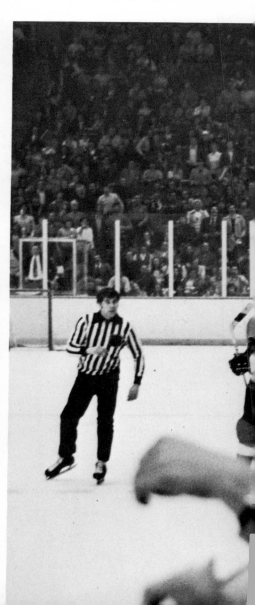

Top: Nystrom pummels Schultz. *Above:* Baited in the penalty box. *Opposite:* "Hound" Kelly on the loose.

pads; a spectator's anticipation of an explosion grows subconsciously to a breaking point. When the players fight, the fan's emotions are swept along with the battle. Thousands would not go home consciously disappointed if the tensions of a good hockey game failed to erupt in fisticuffs, but no one feels let down if they do. It seems to be a natural resolution, and it can be mesmerizing. Says Flyers coach Fred Shero, "All those people who complain about the violence—do you ever see them run out of the building when the game gets rough?"

It can be a great show, but enjoying it is not just a matter of sitting back and watching. First, some deep inhibitions have to be shed. Taught from childhood that respectable people shouldn't enjoy this sort of thing, adult fans apparently need an excuse to let themselves go. After attending an Islanders-Flyers game, New York psychoanalyst Ted Saretsky commented, "My impression during the game was that the crowd wanted the Islanders to be pushed around by the Flyers. I saw that hockey crowd hoping in a primitive way for the Flyers to commit an act that would represent an indignity to the Islanders; to create a feeling of self-righteousness that the fans could identify with."

According to Saretsky, the fans root as much for the oppressors as for the oppressed. "Even though the fans seem to be rooting for the underdog to slay the bad guys," Saretsky observed, "they also seem to have a vicarious identification with the bad guys to brutalize and get away with it. In our society, there aren't too many opportunities for a guy like Dave Schultz to be walking the streets, pushing people around, because he would be arrested."

In his own way, Schultz recognizes the fans' desire for him to be the agent of aggression. "It's weird," he says. "When we skate onto the ice in somebody else's building we can almost *feel* the fans waiting for us to get into some fights. The feeling is so strong that sometimes you almost feel obligated to start something, as if that's what they paid their money to come and see."

As insecure as the fans are the owners, who are reluctant to admit that, in part, they are marketing the kamikaze tactics of a Keith Magnuson, the bullying of a Dave Schultz, or the punching speed and power of a Dan Maloney. Most owners seem to feel that selling such a product lowers them to the status of the local wrestling or roller derby promoter.

The supposedly higher-class operators, who claim to put less emphasis on violent fouling and fighting, have been known to publicly scorn the clubs that sell it more openly. When the Philadelphia Flyers went bullyish in 1972–73, Emile Francis, coach and general manager of the New York Rangers, commented, "No doubt about it; they were looking for the two-dollar ticket. I call it Eastern League Hockey. [The old Eastern League was a lower-class minor league, notorious for its crude play.] Everybody in Halloween masks and all out for roller derby. It's like the lions and the tigers under the big top. I've seen other teams do it. Chicago did it about fifteen years ago. Then it was the Boston Bruins, and now it's the Flyers.''

Francis no doubt regretted his deprecatory remarks when the Flyers beat his Rangers in the Stanley Cup semifinals of 1973–74, and finished 25 points ahead of them in the Patrick Division of the Clarence Campbell Conference in 1974–75. The scorning, if not the criticizing of the Flyers, has markedly decreased since they became a championship team. Nevertheless, it is not every coach who will defend the roughhousing as pointedly as the Flyers' Fred Shero. "If it's pretty skating they want to see," he says gruffly, "let 'em go to the Ice Capades.''

The rule of thumb seems to be that violence becomes brutality only when it victimizes the home team; otherwise it's healthy aggressiveness.

Not very far beneath all the inhibitions and self-serving accusations lies the inescapable fact that the violence occasionally turns ugly. It takes great ethical flexibility to enjoy the entertaining aspects of the violence and then disassociate oneself from the serious injuries that it can cause. Murray Oliver, the man who finally pulled Dave Forbes off Henry Boucha, remembers, "When Henry and Forbes had their original fight, the fans loved it. Then they were sent to the penalty box for seven minutes and kept arguing back and forth, and the fans loved that too. Then Forbes jumped Henry, they saw all the blood, and they didn't like it anymore. They wanted to lynch the guy. I think it's the same with fans all over the league: a little blood, some stitches, no big deal. But too much blood and they don't like it at all.''

The dilemma is even more acute for reporters and broadcasters, some of whom have taken upon themselves the delicate task of entertaining their audience with lighthearted commentary on the subculture of hockey violence while at the same time deploring the rising tide of violence in pro sports. Consider the following column on the Philadelphia Flyers by Jim Murray of the Los Angeles *Times:*

Never go into the corners of a hockey rink with members of the Philadelphia Flyers. Part of you may never come out.

The Flyers are a hockey team whose strategy and tactics are right out of the German Luftwaffe. They rule by terror. They should drop leaflets before they take the ice.

There are better skaters in the league, better scorers, better defenses, but there are no better bullies. Every man in the lineup is a rubber-hose man at heart. They collect at a fight in swarms. Even the fans aren't safe. They went into the seats after the customers in Vancouver last year. They have the reputation of guys who would release the brakes on a baby carriage on a hill over a river. They say before the Flyers sign a man they put him alone in a room with a bobcat and he doesn't come out until he makes it meow.

Some years ago, when there was another of the periodic outcries over "violence that is ruining hockey," Major Conn Smythe, then owner of the Toronto Maple

Leafs, said, "Well, we're going to have to stamp this out or people are going to keep buying tickets." In that pre-PR era, Smythe clearly had no illusions about the nature of the product he was selling. His philosophy remains privately respected, if not publicly respectable, among owners today. Much as one reaches for a couple of aspirins to cure a headache, hockey owners like to pop a few headhunters into their lineups whenever they feel the migraine of a losing team—and the consequent poor attendance. The Los Angeles Kings toughened up their image and increased their box office appeal with the addition of Dan Maloney and Terry Harper. Likewise, the Pittsburgh Penguins started drawing larger and more

War and peace: Bruins' John McKenzie displayed signs of both, but was a more convincing warrior than flower child.

enthusiastic crowds after they obtained Steve Durbano, and Bob ("Battleship") Kelly.

For all its speed and flair, its poetic grace and beauty, hockey is a game that—everything else being equal—the meanest team wins. Violent fouling, and frequently the mere threat of it (intimidation), can subdue an opposing team every bit as effectively as textbook forechecking and backchecking. Add talent and desire to the intimidation, and the rewards can be handsome.

The Boston Bruins of the last decade are a good example of a team that rose with roughhousing and declined without it. After setting a club record of almost 1,300 penalty minutes in the 1968–69 season, when they finished second and lost a stirring playoff semifinal series to Montreal, the Bruins became as well known for their marauding style as they were for the individual heroics of Bobby Orr and Phil Esposito. "The Big Bad Bruins," as they were called, were a bold, brash, totally irreverent band of troublemakers. "Just a bunch of kooks and degenerates who get along," said Eddie Johnston, one of their goaltenders.

"It all began in training camp in sixty-seven," recalls Derek Sanderson, now with the Rangers. "Teddy Green was one tough gent, and in training camp that year he said he was tired of fighting alone. He said that he'd better start getting some help on the ice or there was going to be hell to pay in our dressing room. Teddy had this way of staring at you, this long, cold, hard, deep stare. Well, before you knew it, everybody on the team was a fighter."

Like a shipload of sailors on shore leave, the Bruins brawled their way to the Stanley Cup in 1970—their first Cup in 29 years. When they captured both the East Division title (their first in 30 years) and the Stanley Cup in 1971–72, the Bruins appeared to be on the verge of a dynasty. Then, in the summer of 1972, the WHA raided them for Green, Sanderson, and John MacKenzie. When Boston reported to training camp that fall, much of the talent was still there, but the barroom swagger was gone, and with it went Boston's ability to intimidate others. The Bruins have not been the same team since.

"The Bruins drew strength from each other, especially at home," says Pat Quinn, the big Atlanta defenseman who, as a member of the Toronto Maple Leafs, was involved in several memorable brawls in Boston Garden. "John MacKenzie was chippy, a real agitator, and he

Bruins' Fred O'Donnell lunges for the jugular of Rod
Seiling. When the Rangers were perennial bridesmaids
to Boston in the East Division, critics charged New
York was intimidated. The image still lingers.

98

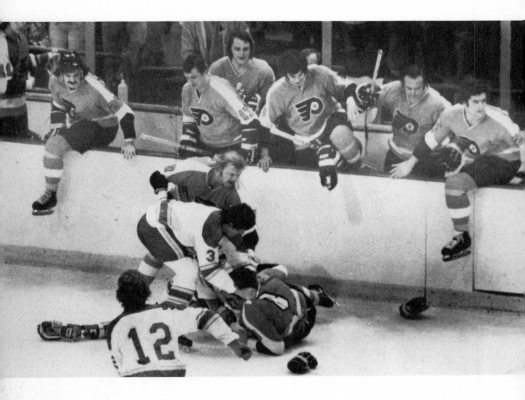

had a lot to do with their success. By himself he was nothing, but he knew—and so did you—that anytime he started something the rest of the team would be right at his elbow. Whenever you took on one of those Bruins, you knew you'd have a gang of them all over you before it was finished."

Sticking together is still the rule among intimidating hockey clubs, even though the third-man rule has limited the overt gang warfare. (The third-man rule mandates the referee to issue a match penalty to any player who joins a fight between two men.) Third-man rule or no, the tough teams are not going to stand around and watch if one of their own is taking a licking. Quinn says of the Flyers, "Those guys really stick together. You get into a fight with one of them, and they have guys throwing pucks at you from the bench."

On every good club there is at least one man whose unofficial duty is to prevent opposing players from bully-

Methods of intimidation. *Above:* When the Flyers lose one-on-one, they resort to gang warfare. Flames' Pat Quinn is the victor-soon-to-be-victim. *Opposite:* Canadiens' John Ferguson did fine on his own—witness this thrashing of Reg Fleming.

ing his teammates. However, these "policemen" are not likely to wait for an assault to take place before attacking. One example of this was Montreal's John Ferguson. When he was brought up from Cleveland in 1963, Ferguson was not the high-scoring forward the opposition had learned to expect in a Canadiens uniform. His primary mission in Montreal was to accomplish with his fists what he could not with orthodox talent. Only minutes into his first NHL game, against Boston, he picked a fight with Green. After Ferguson won that fight and others, opponents became reluctant to rough up smaller Montreal players for fear of having to deal with him. As a result, the Canadiens were given more freedom to capitalize on their many and varied talents. (Ferguson himself developed into a 30-goal scorer.)

Below: Ted Lindsay swipes at Zellio Toppazzini. A small man, Lindsay found that his stick was "the great equalizer," but he could fight without it, too. *Opposite:* He fends off Bruins' Bob Armstrong.

"When I became coach of the Bruins," recalls general manager Harry Sinden, "I would have taken John Ferguson over anybody in the league—*anybody*. His aggressiveness could lift an entire team and keep it hitting and fighting long after it had passed the point of exhaustion."

When he returned to the Red Wings in 1964, at age 39,
Lindsay was as crafty as ever with the blade. Chicago's
Bill Hay experienced the Lindsay backchecking style.

"I hated to play against Fergie," says Brad Park, who as a right defenseman for the New York Rangers frequently went into the corners with Ferguson, a left winger. "Fergie loved to make you eat crow. He was always there, elbows up, crowding you, messing up your game. After a while you'd think about dropping the gloves and getting him off your back, but at the same time you knew that wouldn't make anyone happier than Fergie. He was one of the best fighters in the league, and he looked forward to a good go now and then. I fought Fergie a number of times and wondered if it was worth it. Without a doubt, he had a lot to do with the success of the Canadiens."

Ted Lindsay was one of the most violent players in the NHL and also one of the most successful, lasting 17 years in the league, most of them as a member of the famed "Production Line," with Gordie Howe and Sid Abel.

Today his face remains a quilt of deep scars and hasty stitchwork, his reward for challenging every foe. After playing what were supposed to be his last three years in the NHL with the Chicago Black Hawks, Lindsay suddenly decided to end a four-year retirement for the 1964–65 season, "just so I could say I finished my career with the Red Wings." Lindsay was 39 years old at the time, but as the season unfolded, it became obvious that he had not mellowed with age. In a game at Montreal he speared defenseman Ted Harris, who stood seven inches taller and outweighed him by forty pounds. When the Canadiens' Claude Larose tried to intervene on Harris' behalf, Lindsay sent him off the ice with a wicked two-hander across the legs. In that, his final season, Lindsay again finished among the league leaders in penalties, and Detroit won its first regular season title in eight years.

Lindsay says he was after an edge on the opposition, however slight. Perhaps it was an extra split second to make a pass, or to get off a good shot, or to gain control of the puck in a corner. If an opposing player had the puck, Lindsay wanted him to worry about where Lindsay was and what he might do, thereby making it difficult for him to concentrate on finding an open man with a pass or picking a corner of the net with his shot.

Today, Lindsay leaves no doubt that he bent the rules to accomplish his mission. "Personally, my style was using my stick with a little bit of a hook, a little bit of a slash, to gain an advantage on my opponent," he says. "I was a little guy [5 feet 8 inches, 160 pounds] and things didn't come so easily for me. . . . My stick was the great equalizer."

Former referee Bill Chadwick is more blunt: "Lindsay was plain *mean*. If he had to play dirty to win, he played dirty."

Obviously, the so-called policemen do a lot more than protect their teammates. They don't wait to be challenged before beginning their illegal intimidation tactics —they issue the challenges, and then seize on the slightest retaliation as a justification to drop the gloves. They have no use for lawyerlike distinctions between what is and what isn't legal. Call it healthy aggressiveness (as they do) or illegal aggression (as their critics do), their style of play intimidates opponents and wins hockey games.

It is a philosophy accepted by fighters and nonfighters alike. "I'm not a fighter," says Murray Oliver, who, despite his size (5 feet 9 inches, 170 pounds), has lasted 17 years in the NHL. "If I had tried to fight my way into the NHL I'd have been killed before I even got here. Fighting and intimidation isn't my nature, but at the same time I can appreciate the value of intimidation. A team can get a lot done against an opponent that it has intimidated."

"Look at it this way," said the Minnesota North Stars' Dennis Hextall one afternoon, sitting in the lobby of a Detroit motel. "Tonight we're playing the Red Wings, and when I look across the ice there will be eighteen guys in red and white sweaters on their bench. If I've got six of them scared, I've only got to beat twelve, right? So rubbing people is my game. A glove in the face, a whack at the ankles, elbows up—stuff like that. When I'm playing a physical game, maybe I can incite someone into taking a cheap penalty. Maybe I can draw a guy out of position and set up a goal. When I'm rubbing people out there, things happen. When I'm not, I stink."

In January, 1971, in a game against the Canadiens in Montreal, Hextall started rubbing Canadiens after they had built a 3–0 lead in two periods. When the game was over, he had the entire Montreal team taking runs at him and forgetting the other North Stars and the puck. Minnesota tied the game 3–3 on a goal set up by Hextall, whose own goal had made the score 3–2.

"When I'm rubbing people, things happen. When I'm not, I stink," confesses hit man Dennis Hextall. By pausing in his work, Hextall appears to be doing the linesman a favor.

When Hextall fell into disfavor with Minnesota management toward the end of the 1974–75 season, the Flyers' Fred Shero let it be known that he was interested in obtaining the player's services. "He's one of the three most·competitive players I've ever coached," the Flyers' coach says. "The year I had him at Buffalo we set a record for victories on the road by an AHL team, and Hextall was the reason why."

Shero, the chief apostle of intimidation, credits a single act of it with the Flyers' win of the Stanley Cup in 1974.

It took place at Boston Garden in the second game of the series between the Flyers and the Bruins. After winning the first game 3–2, the Bruins opened up a quick 2–0 lead in the second game. Bobby Clarke cut the Flyers' deficit to one goal with a score at 1:08 of the second period, and the Flyers' Andre Dupont sent the game into overtime with a goal only 52 seconds from the end of regulation play.

At 12:01 of the first overtime period, Clarke got the Flyers the one game they had to win in Boston, converting a pass from Bill Flett after Dave Schultz had stolen the puck from two Bruins in the left corner. The Flyers went on to win the series, four games to two, after which Boston coach Bep Guidolin lamented, "We left the series in that overtime. That evened up the series with a game apiece, and all they had to do was win their games in Philadelphia. If we had won that overtime game, we would have won the Cup."

Almost a year later, Shero reflected on that key overtime victory while discussing the merits of intimidation over a Michelob in St. Louis' Chase Park Plaza Hotel. "When you come to intimidation I think, yes, Mr. Schultz won the Stanley Cup for us," he said. "During all twenty minutes of the third period I didn't put him on the ice. I was afraid he might get a cheap penalty. But the fans kept harassing me. 'We want Schultz! We want Schultz!'

"I got fed up and said, 'Get out there.' Well, he jumped on the ice on the fly and there were two big Boston players in the corner. He went straight from our bench into that corner, and those two big Boston players jumped out of his way. Schultz passed out to Bill Flett, who gave it to Clarke, and the game was over.

"Schultz didn't even touch those two players. They just jumped out of the way. I couldn't believe it when they left that puck—right in Boston. So many clubs are tough only in their own rinks, but Schultz gives us courage on the road. You can't measure the value of a man like that."

In Schultz, the Flyers have the most celebrated (and penalized) hit man in hockey history, but his most significant characteristic is not all his penalties and his notoriety, but the fact that in many respects he sets the style for the whole team. The Flyers have at least half a dozen others for whom legality is anything they can get away with, the more audaciously intimidating, the better. Philadelphia is a good team not simply because it is a bruising one—it is also the most disciplined team in pro hockey today, with perhaps the finest goaltender, Bernie Parent. The Flyers are closely knit and as highly motivated as any team. Nevertheless, as the Canadiens have come to symbolize speed and fluidity in hockey, the Flyers are the symbols of violence and extralegal intimidation—a well-deserved reputation. Theirs is a strategy based not only on hard work, disciplined positional play, and crunching body contact, but also on testing and breaking the rules in an attempt to stifle the opposition. The Flyers have mastered the intimidation game, and they force every opponent to master it also before they

The bedrock of the Flyers' success is their goalie, Bernie Parent. In a rare lapse, Philadelphia defense allows Bob Nystrom through—but Parent has him covered.

allow the game to be contested on more respectable grounds.

The Flyers have always relied on defense and goal-tending. But in their early years, they suffered the stigma of a team that could be cowed. The St. Louis Blues, in particular, made a practice of beating the Flyers by out-muscling them. In *The Broad Street Bullies,* Jack Chevalier recounts the time in 1973–74 that St. Louis bad-guy-turned-broadcaster, Noel Picard, asked his intermission guest, Simon Nolet, an original Flyer, why the two teams had had so many fights. " 'You ought to know, Noel,' " Nolet answered, 'You started 'em all.' " (The Flyers' record against the Blues was 4–20–8 from 1968–69 to 1971–72.)

"I can remember when I was coaching the Flyers and was embarrassed to take them into Boston and St. Louis," says Keith Allen, who as general manager acquired every player on the present team. "Those players knew they would get the hell kicked out of them back then. Half of them didn't even want to go on the ice. We decided to fight fire with fire."

After the Flyers bowed out of the 1969 playoffs by surrendering four straight games to the then-belligerent St. Louis Blues, owner Ed Snider, realizing that his team had been intimidated, decided to "put an emphasis on size." That year the Flyers drafted (in addition to Bobby Clarke) Dave Schultz and Don Saleski, both heavy-weights. The next year the Flyers selected Bob Kelly. Within two years all three were with the parent club, and the Flyers began winning.

The man most responsible for changing the Flyers' image is their coach and master strategist since 1971–72, Fred Shero. A diminutive, dapper man, with smoked-lens glasses and a thick dark mustache, Shero reminds many people of Dr. Strangelove. In reality, he is nothing so exotic. Although he is subject to flights of fancy, he is a hard-nosed product of a hard-nosed system. Shero spent two and a half years as a mediocre defenseman with the New York Rangers, then turned to coaching, at which he did much better. In 13 years in the minors, mostly in the Rangers' organization, his team finished first five times, second and third once each. In 1970–71, the year before he joined Philadelphia, his Omaha team won the league championship in the Central Hockey League, and then captured the Jack Adams Trophy by defeating the Dallas Black Hawks in the playoff finals.

Behind the bench, Fred Shero can be the traditional tough coach. But his genius lies in challenging traditional approaches to the game and its players.

Shero contends that whatever strategy of intimidation the Flyers have is rooted in their personalities. He boasts that they are dedicated to doing anything that can help the team win, and that this dedication makes them fearless. He takes little credit for the resource—he claims merely to utilize it. That day at the Chase Park Plaza, Shero reflected at length about the tactics and personality of his team and his role in shaping them.

I've never in my life asked a player to go out and start a fight. In training camp I tell my team if I ever ask you to start a fight I want you to break that stick over my head. As a player I lost my job in the big leagues because I wouldn't fight. I can't; it's not in my nature to attack another man. He has to throw the first punch. That's why I was sent down. I don't think I had five fights in my entire playing career, and I didn't initiate one of them.

I've coached for eighteen years, on just about every level of professional hockey. I've had teams that you might say were chicken. They wouldn't fight, but that was their nature, and you're not going to change it. . . . If a man doesn't have courage, I just don't think you're going to develop it. You've got to be abrasive by nature. We've got guys like Schultz, Dupont, Kelly, Saleski. They don't win all their fights but they'll fight and fight again. It's their nature. . . .

A lot of people don't realize, and neither do a lot of hockey

"Aggressive by nature," according to coach Shero, Don Saleski expects to take a few hits as well as to issue them. *Right:* He sheds Bill Hogaboam. *Opposite:* Larry Carriere sheds him.

players, that there are four corners in a rink. And there are two pits—one in front of your net and one in front of theirs. A lot of players don't have the courage to go into those corners and those pits. They'll go in halfheartedly or they'll arrive late. Well, my team *arrives.* No matter how small a man is, he's going to fight honestly for that puck; sometimes this creates friction that can result in a fight, but that's part of the game. My system demands that you go in front of the net, and even though two men may be hitting you illegally from behind, you've got to hold your ground. Sometimes *this* results in a fight.

In the end it gets back to courage. This whole team has more than any other I've ever coached.

Courage is the most respectable product of the Flyers' total dedication to victory, and their coach loves to emphasize it, often by rationalizing the inevitable excesses. "Sure, we get more penalties than anybody else," Shero admits, "but it's only because we're playing the game the way it should be played."

This is as close as Shero comes to admitting that the Flyers' game plan includes violent fouling. Traditionally, a team will knowingly take the initiative in breaking the rules only when it is desperate to prevent a score. Shero implicitly advocates a strategy of "aggressive" fouls as well.

On May 7, 1975, at the Nassau Coliseum, in the fourth game of their semifinal series with the New York

Fred Shero preaches that the most telling battles occur in the corners and in the pits—the area directly in front of the net. Bob Kelly wins this battle with a woodchopper's blow to the helmet of Bob Gainey.

Referee observes Flyers' Tom Bladon rub Flames' Bennett. Called for so many obvious fouls, the Flyers also get away with more than any other team.

Islanders, the Flyers found themselves trailing 3–0 halfway through the game. After a relatively even first period, the Flyers were obviously lagging in the second. When the Islanders scored their third goal, at 12:49, Shero sent Schultz over the boards, and the Flyers' bad man charged directly at his opposite number on the Islanders, Garry Howatt. Shero may not have told Schultz to start a fight, but Schultz didn't have to be told. With no pretext of a provocation, he pounded Howatt into the boards, and the two began fighting. The Islanders' fans responded by joining the mayhem, screaming and throwing debris at Schultz. When order was finally restored, referee Dave Newell penalized Howatt five minutes for fighting and Schultz five minutes for fighting with an additional two minutes for provoking the brawl.

The Flyers lost the battle of the penalties, but almost

won the war. Whether it was the stoppage in play or the fact that the Islanders felt safe with their 3–0 lead, the New Yorkers failed to press their one-man advantage, and the Flyers easily killed the penalty, breaking the Islanders' momentum. Soon, the Islanders were making careless errors, and the Flyers capitalized, scoring two goals before the end of the second period. In the third period, the Flyers got the tying goal and completely dominated the play, outshooting the Islanders 13–3 and only narrowly missing the winning goal when Reggie Leach scored, a second after the third period ended.

The Islanders rallied and won the game in sudden-death overtime, deflecting public attention from the Flyers' comeback, but not changing the fact that the reversal that was central to the game was obviously precipitated by the Schultz-Howatt incident. Schultz didn't intimidate Howatt or the Islanders, and he probably didn't spark the Flyers, but he did provide the Islanders with what seemed like an opportunity to relax. When they did, their lapse was almost fatal. Ironically, had Schultz not been more heavily penalized than Howatt, the Islanders might not have taken it easy and lost their edge.

By taking as well as provoking penalties, the Flyers can break the discipline of a less violent team, even without intimidation. The profusion of penalties can disrupt a team's rhythm, perhaps by scrambling set line combinations or by reducing the game to four-on-four situations, which tend to encourage free skating over close checking. Unlike other teams that have favored the tough style, the Flyers use this breakdown in discipline not to score enough goals to provide a cushion for a sloppy defense, but to facilitate their tight checking. Says Shero, "When we're ahead three–one, it's not going to wind up seven–five. We are not going to trade goals and just make sure we're ahead at the end of the game."

The Bruins of the late sixties, and the Penguins of the seventies, surrendered a lot of goals in the expectation that by outmuscling the opposition they could score even more. The Flyers' game plan is never to lose their discipline while provoking opponents into losing theirs.

Of course, it helps not to get caught, and the Flyers, though they are the most heavily penalized team in hockey, are also undoubtedly the team that gets away with the most. Like the Russians, they are famous for blurring the already fine line between incidental contact and interference (the techniques for which they are said to sharpen in practice). They are also experts at holding, hooking, elbowing, and cross-checking in a style innocent enough to avoid a penalty. Although each incident appears almost insignificant, the cumulative effect leaves the Flyers' opponents exhausted and frustrated.

Basically, this is the classic clutch-and-grab style of hockey—well known in pro hockey for decades—but the Flyers are particularly adept at it because of their willingness to commit blatant fouls as well. With referees reluctant to overburden the game with penalties, the Flyers' blatant fouls, for which they are caught, tend to camouflage the less obvious ones.

Denis Potvin of the New York Islanders says, ''If the Flyers commit a hundred and fifty violations, it is obvious that a referee cannot call all of them, or he will make

Reputed to keep his stick on the ice only if he has to play the puck, veteran defenseman Ed Van Impe is one of the Flyers' craftiest foulers. Dave Keon is the victim of this assault.

himself and the game look ridiculous. So he overlooks a lot of them, and the easiest ones to overlook are the late hits, the grabbing, the hooking with a stick. You wear out a lot faster when somebody is holding and clutching you the whole game, and you become very angry and distracted."

In short, many of the Flyers' fouls go unpenalized, and the relatively small cumulative cost of the penalties they do take is a modest price to pay for using border-line and downright illegal tactics to control the corners and the "pits." Naturally, the Flyers' opponents react by fouling and fighting more themselves, only to learn that the Flyers are hard to beat at the violence game. They have one of the league's more potent power plays, scoring more power-play goals than their opponents on far

fewer opportunities. Moreover, because the Flyers are so well balanced, they can easily replace almost any man they lose because of penalties, whereas their opponents often rely heavily on a particular man. It is often this man that the Flyers succeed in engaging in battle and removing from the ice.

The Flyers are not the first nor will they be the last team to use excessive violence as a tactic, but they may very well be the best, because instead of using it to compensate for their deficiencies—of which they have very few—they make it supplement their strengths. They have mastered the basic skills of hockey, and violence gives them the extra edge. Without it they would be a good team; with it they are champions.

Removing the opponent's big man is part of the Flyers' strategy. *Above:* Moose Dupont tangles with Brad Park. *Opposite:* The inevitable result.

4.
The Breeding
of Toughness

When Gordie Howe signed as a 16-year-old with the Detroit Red Wings in 1944, he got $4,500. When 18-year-old Wilf Paiement signed with the Kansas City Scouts in 1974, he got $600,000 over three years. Howe played his first pro season with Omaha, in the United States Hockey League. Paiement played his first pro *game* in the National Hockey League, in Toronto's Maple Leaf Gardens.

With NHL and World Hockey Association teams scattered across the United States, more American boys than ever before are playing hockey, and like their Canadian counterparts, they harbor dreams of playing in the big leagues. But the breeding of professional hockey players—witness Wilf Paiement—is a process that remains solidly entrenched in the traditions of provincial Canada, a country that, as Toronto author Scott Young recently observed, "still is engaged in pushing back its fierce and beautiful frontiers."

The increased demand for hockey talent has accelerated the progress of young players to the major league level and changes many of them once they arrive, but the formative years of today's hockey players remain similar to those of the old-timers. Amid the restructuring of major league hockey, the all-out assault on its records, and the affluence and security of modern players, the breeding of the players themselves is hockey's link with its past.

Wilf Paiement has yet to reach his twentieth birthday. After growing up in Earlton, Ontario, he left home at fifteen to play Junior A hockey for Niagara Falls of the Ontario Hockey Association. He played the next two years for St. Catharines, and after scoring 50 goals and 73 assists in 1973–74, he was the number-one draft choice of the new Kansas City franchise in the NHL.

Before signing, he provoked three months of the most intensive bargaining in the history of professional hockey. At the conclusion of the amateur draft, Alan Eagleson, Paiement's attorney, had predicted that the youth would receive the biggest contract ever offered a Junior hockey player. He was right.

On September 6, only eight days before the Scouts opened training camp in Port Huron, Michigan, Paiement signed his contract and was introduced to Kansas City amid the clutter of glaring television lights, whirring cameras, microphones, and reporters' notepads. General manager Sid Abel said that the rookie would be assigned

At the signing. Left to right: G. Robert Fisher, Scouts' lawyer; Ed Watters, associate of Paiement's agen Alan Eagleson; Wilf; Edwin Thompson, club president.

number nine, which had been worn with distinction by such NHL stars as Gordie Howe, Bobby Hull, and Maurice Richard.

Most critics agree that Paiement is destined to become a star. He skates with the strong, fluid strides of a Howe. His shot is hard, fast, and heavy. Around the net he has a "goal sense" that cannot be taught: in his rookie year he produced 26 goals.

"Our scout in St. Catharines, Fred Litzen, had known Wilf since he was sixteen and he couldn't say enough about him," says Abel. "At that time we didn't know if the NHL would be drafting underage Juniors. But Litzen said that if the league did, Wilf had to be our number one."

Finally, and most to the point, Paiement is tough. He is a 6-foot 190-pounder who blends raw talent with great strength, fearlessness, and resolve. "What we especially liked was the kid's toughness and aggressiveness in the corners," Abel continues. "You don't find that very often today. He's definitely an 'old school' player."

According to the coach of the Montreal Canadiens, Scotty Bowman, "The kid's got to be tough. He comes from the north country."

The north country is the vast, timber-laden reaches of northern Ontario and Quebec, where the people are as rugged as the land. Their work days begin before sunrise and end after sundown. Through the splendid

summers and bitter cold winters, they live by mining gold, zinc, and copper, and by cutting down huge trees for the lumber camps and the paper mills. Farther north, along the shores of James Bay and Hudson Bay in Quebec, trappers set their snares for mink, beaver, fox, and chinchilla.

To the St. Louis Blues' Bob Plager, a native of the area, the north country means "cold, cold, and gold. It's so far north we have eight months of snow and four months of bad sledding. The temperature dips to sixty below, but you don't feel it—you're frozen."

Like the rest of life in the north country, relaxation takes people outdoors, hunting for moose and white-tailed deer in the forests, lying in wait for ducks and geese near the water, or fishing for pike, trout, whitefish, and bass in the lakes and streams. One of the few concessions to indoor sport is the local hotel or tavern, where townspeople drain tall green bottles of Labatt's or Molson, enjoying the wallop of seven percent alcohol.

Wilf Paiement, Jr., is the youngest of the 16 children of Wilfred and Rosila Paiement of Earlton, a tiny, French-speaking community a few miles west of the Quebec border. One of Paiement's older brothers, Larry, an excellent hockey player, was drafted by the Boston Bruins, but opted for the home and hearth life of the local area. Another brother, Rosaire, spent five years with Philadelphia and Vancouver of the NHL before he jumped to the WHA.

The elder Paiement, now sixty-six years old, has never played hockey, but he has passed down to his sons a stern philosophy of life that finds expression on a hockey rink as suitably as in the wilds of the north country. The children greatly respect their father, as indeed do many other people in the north country. He lost his farm during the Depression but fought back through lumbering, farming, construction, and horse trading. Today, he owns thirty-eight hundred acres of timber, farmland, and other real estate in and around Earlton, runs a flourishing construction company that employs two of his sons (Larry and Ambrose) full-time, and owns a stable of trotters that he races regularly at tracks in Quebec City and Montreal. More than for his wealth, however, Wilfred Paiement, Sr., is known for his feats of strength.

"When I was twelve years old, I used to take on anybody in northern Ontario and northern Quebec who

Wilf in action. *Top:* First goal ever scored at Crosby Kemper Memorial Arena. *Bottom:* Beating Rangers' Sanderson and leading the rush.

From the Paiement album. *Clockwise from top:*
Family portrait taken before Wilf Jr. was born;
lumberjack and wife; big and little Wilf;
Rosie the hockey player; at Batavia Downs;
horse breeder, family man.

wanted to arm wrestle," he remembers. "Some men weighed two hundred twenty-five pounds, but I wrestled them all." In 1933, at age 24, he crushed the hand of Paul LaTour, the champion of northern Quebec; forty years later he defeated a 296-pound wrestler and weight-lifter from Boston who underestimated the strength of a sixty-three-year-old man.

In 1939, Wilfred Paiement wrestled a 700-pound brown bear before 18,000 people in the Quebec City Coliseum, and left the bear sprawled on the mat, its tongue blue as ink. The next year, while working as a contractor for the A. J. Murphy Lumber Company, Paiement put 14 men in the hospital after a wild brawl over a pay dispute.

Sitting at the kitchen table in his son's North Kansas City apartment, Wilf, Sr., recounted his story to the respectful but insistent promptings of Wilf, Jr., whose blue eyes sparkled with enthusiasm for tales he had obviously heard many times but wanted to hear again.

Wilfred Paiement, Sr., came from a family of four brothers and five sisters in St. Sauveur-des-Monts, Quebec, in the Laurentian Mountain area, north of Montreal. His wife came from a family of 18 children. Paiement's parents, farmers and lumber workers, moved to Earlton in 1917, when Wilfred was eight years old.

"I work hard all my life," the elder Paiement began. "I go out in the bush and cut the trees down, bring them to the saw mill and dress the lumber, and send it to Toronto and Montreal. When I was twelve years old, I weigh one hundred and seventy pounds. Up at five, to bed at ten-thirty. Work long hours, all the time. I was a strong boy."

Wilfred and Rosila Paiement were married in 1929, when he was 20 and she 15. After losing their first farm at the outset of the Depression, they managed to start another, clearing the land where the Earlton airport now stands. "In 1930 all her and I had to live on was three dollars and seventy-five cents for two weeks," Paiement recalls. "I could get few jobs, and when I did, it was only fifty cents a day. All we had were the four cows that my father gave us—those cows, a few pigs, and chickens."

In 1930, Rosila Paiement had her first child, Marie Paul. A year later, another girl, Ramon, was born, and in 1932, the first boy, Ambrose.

By 1940, the A. J. Murphy Lumber Company, with Wilfred Paiement as its contractor, was employing 500 men in the forests of northern Ontario. Most of these men were from the Gaspé Peninsula of northeastern Quebec, where many had been out of work and starving. "The Gaspé guys were husky men," Paiement recalls. "They were real mean, those guys—dirty, and dirty talking. They were always drinking the St. Pierre et Miquelon liquor, real white lightning."

One night in October, almost seventy-five of the men came to the makeshift office in the middle of the camp. They were in a surly mood. While most of them milled about restlessly outside, a dozen or so stormed into the small office, demanding more pay.

The Murphy brothers spoke no French, and in any case were not eager to deal with a band of ill-tempered laborers. They told Paiement to inform the men that they could not meet their demands. Paiement relayed the message and told the men at the office to return to the bunkhouses and tell the others. Anybody who was unhappy should show up in the morning—he would pay them off, and they could leave.

Paiement vividly remembers their reaction. "They yelled, 'We will see you in the morning. We are going back to the bunkhouses and tell the rest, and we'll all be back in the morning, and we are going to throw you all in the lake.'

"The Murphy brothers told me to send my wife down to Haileybury, about twenty miles away, to bring back the police," Paiement continues. " 'Don't worry about it,' I said, 'I will handle this myself. Goddamm Gaspé. I will be here in the morning to clean up what we have to clean up. I don't need an army to handle those guys.' "

Paiement returned to the office at three in the morning, wearing knee-high boots with spikes on the soles. When his wife arrived at five, he was lying on the bunk, trying to get some sleep. A half hour later, they could hear the sound of men thrashing through the forest.

No sooner had Paiement told his wife and the other office workers to go to a room in the back of the office than the front door flew open and fifteen men stormed in. The rest waited outside, yelling.

"One of those guys said, 'Where is that goddamm slob, that *enfant chienne* Paiement? He is a coward. He must have disappeared.'

"Now I'm angry. 'Hey, who said that? Who said Paiement was a goddamm coward? *Tell* me. Who's that guy?'

"The leader of the Gaspé guys, he was named Timothy Dumont, a powerful man with a long, hooked nose. He came over and said, 'I'm the guy.'

" 'Listen, my baby,' I told him, 'you are not dealing with a kid this time. You have to be careful what you say.'

In an instant Paiement's right hand clutched Dumont's throat. Dumont lurched backward, dragging the 220-pound Paiement through the door, into the yard outside. One man, wielding a two-by-four, approached from the left. Paiement snatched the piece of lumber with his left hand. Holding Dumont by the neck with his right hand, he slammed him to the ground.

"I lift him and throw him down, and every time I had him down I kick him. When he is unconscious, I grab a kingbolt. It is two feet long, three inches in diameter, and has a long chain on the end. It weighs about seventy pounds. 'Now you're all dead,' I say, and I begin swinging that kingbolt around my head.

"Well, the men all ran into the bush, except for Dumont and thirteen others. They would fall down, and I would jump on top of them. Dumont was injured the worst. He had a broken collar bone, broken ribs, a broken hip, and a broken leg. He was in the hospital for a long time."

Thirty-four years later, Wilfred Paiement broke into a wide grin recalling the incident. "In 1950," he remembered, "we had gone to Gaspé to sell some horses. I was forty-one years old then. After we had sold them at the racetrack there, we stopped to get some gas. I went into the restaurant to pay for the gas, and when I did, I could see some faces in there that I remembered.

"Two men started laughing, and when I saw them, I said, 'Listen, you guys. What are you laughing about? Are you laughing at me, or with me, or what about?'

"I went over to their table and one of the men asked me, 'Are you Mr. Paiement from the lumber company in Earlton, in 1940?'

"I said, 'Yes, that's right.'

" 'Well, Mr. Paiement,' he said, 'I am Phillip Dumont. Could you permit me to tell these guys in the restaurant here just what happened at the lumber camp in Earlton in 1940?'

"I said, 'Go ahead and tell them, sure, and tell them the truth.'

"So he told them. He said, 'Mr. Paiement was alone

and there were five hundred of us, and he put fourteen of us in the hospital. That man, he can handle an army.'

" 'You see this scar up here?' he said, and he pointed to a big scar on his face. 'I got my cheekbone broke. I got several ribs broke. I almost got my neck broke. And my brother Timothy, a big guy, two hundred and twenty-eight pounds—he got hurt the worst of all.'

" 'Is that all you want to know?' I said, and he said yes. 'Then all right, let's shake hands,' I said. 'Anytime you come to the north country, come in and see me. By the way, how is Timothy?'

" 'Oh, he's okay now,' he said. 'He can work.'

"So I left there, and when I did, I looked back and I saw those guys talking. Dumont was pointing to his scar. I think they were saying, 'Look at that, I'll bet that old bugger could still give us a rough time.' "

Among the future notables on the 1964–65 Memorial Cup champion Niagara Falls Flyers were Jim Lorentz, top; Rosaire Paiement, just above cup; Gilles Marotte, front-toothless at top right; Derek Sanderson, below cup; Doug Favell, in jacket; and Don Marcotte, above Favell.

When Larry Paiement was about ten years old, his father bought him his first pair of skates. "Larry was a very clever hockey player—strong, afraid of nothing," the father recalls. "He could show some players in the National League some things today, and he is forty years old. Larry was drafted by Hap Emms for Boston to play in Barrie, but he got married at nineteen and did not go. They sent a guy to take him to Boston, but he would not go. He was getting married instead."

Then there was Rosaire, whose entire life was hockey. "Rosie had a tough time," says Paiement. "We were busy all the time and Rosie was always skating on ponds by himself or with other boys his age. Or he'd go to New Liskeard, nineteen miles away, to play hockey. In the big storms, with the rain coming down, he would be hitchhiking to New Liskeard. In the big storms, that little devil was out there on the road with his bag on his shoulder. He was always gone, playing hockey."

With Larry playing in a local league sponsored by the area's merchants, and Rosaire dreaming of a career in the NHL, hockey began to play a strong role in Paiement family life.

"When Wilf was one-and-a-half years old we used to bring him to the hockey games where Larry was playing," the father recalls. "And little Wilf would jump on the ice and run, and whoever was looking after the arena would have to run after him. And he would have trouble catching him too! And Larry would sometimes take Wilf on his shoulder and skate around the rink, oh maybe four or five times, and go like hell."

When he was nine years old, Wilf inherited a pair of skates from Rosaire, who by that time was eighteen. The skates were size nine, too large for the feet of the youngest Paiement, but he used them anyway.

At first, the fun was in skating on a frozen pond, fooling around with a puck at the end of a stick, or playing with kids in a pickup game.

When he was eleven years old, Wilf was taken, by his father and brother Larry, to New Liskeard to play in a game. "I didn't want to go," Wilf recalls. "I didn't know anything about hockey. And those were big guys, grown men. But Larry took me anyway, and when we got there I couldn't even understand what the coach was saying. All I could speak was French. But Larry would translate for me. He said, 'Don't worry. I will play with you. You go park yourself near the net and I will feed you the puck.' I always listened to what Larry said, and that's what I did."

About a month later, the Paiement family watched Larry and Wilf in a game at New Liskeard. After the elder Paiement told a man at the local school that young Wilf would be playing that night, the school bus was filled with kids eager to witness the spectacle. Larry bought them frankfurters, and his father paid for the french fries and ice cream.

"And what a night it was!" recalls the elder Paiement. "Wilf would go park near the net, just like Larry told him to. Then Larry would come up the ice, stickhandle, stickhandle. Then he would give the puck to Wilf and bang!—into the net it would go.

"The bus driver from the school, he was sitting beside me. 'Oh, Mr. Paiement,' he was saying. 'This is wonderful! And Wilf is only eleven years old!'

"One, two, three, four, five goals Wilf got that night, and we won the game five to nothing."

As for Wilf, even this heady experience was not enough to kindle in him the desire to become a pro hockey player. As the youngest in a prospering, if still provincial, family, his life was comfortable and secure.

"When I am nine years old I am driving my father's truck over the back roads, eh, and it is a pretty good life," he says. "When I am fifteen, I have these little calves. I get up at four-thirty in the morning to feed them. I mix water with the powdered milk, feed my calves, then come back and have breakfast. Then I leave for Kirkland Lake, which is thirty miles away. There I am in charge of a crew working for my father. I look after four machines and work the big loader. We are dynamiting these rocks, and when you move those rocks you have to be very careful that you do not cut the tires on your truck. Those rocks are sharp as needles and those tires cost a hundred bucks apiece.

"So we load rocks all day long and at five-thirty everybody else, they can leave. But I stay for another forty-five minutes to gas up the trucks and make sure everything is ready for the next day. Then I drive back home, thirty miles, and I have to feed my calves again, eh? I have dinner about seven-thirty and then I go and maybe play ball. I am in bed about eleven o'clock because I have to get up to feed my calves and go to Kirkland Lake the next day."

If a boy shows any promise by his early teens, he is

The pressures of Junior hockey are intense. Some players sacrifice finishing high school in order to pursue their hockey careers.

invariably offered an opportunity to play Junior B hockey, or, if he is good enough, Junior A. Wilf Paiement was good enough. Hap Emms, the same man who had pursued Larry Paiement fifteen years before, came to Earlton and asked Wilf, then only 15, to play Junior A hockey for him in Niagara Falls, five hundred miles to the southeast.

"He was the baby," recalls Rosila Paiement. "I don't say anything, but I cry. I don't want my baby living away from home. I don't cry in front of Wilfred, but he's so small, you know?"

"He's not really so small then," her husband offers, "but he had the baby heart, you see. . . ."

For many youngsters, playing Junior hockey means leaving home for seven months a year. Bep Guidolin, who is now Paiement's coach at Kansas City, and who spent many years running Junior teams in Oshawa and London, admits that, for the players, Junior hockey is a crash course in self-sufficiency and not all of them pass. "There were dropouts, to be sure," he says. "Homesickness and poor grades were the big reasons.

They played a seventy-game schedule, with overnight bus trips, and a lot of them never finished high school because of it. I mean, when a kid gets home at three or four in the morning, and he's got to get up for school at six or seven, it's not easy."

Paiement had dropped out of school to play Junior hockey, but he had more than average difficulty adjusting to the new life. Most of the other players were English-speaking natives of Ontario, and Paiement spoke only French. Lonely in a strange town, and unable to communicate with people around him, fifteen-year-old Wilf began to wonder whether playing hockey was worth the sacrifices. Even the game itself became a grind.

"They would push you around, try to make you run," he remembers of the competition. "Especially somebody like me, who was only fifteen. The average guy was eighteen years old, and some of them really wanted to make the NHL. Jim Schoenfeld [now with the Buffalo Sabres] was there when I was, and Shonnie really wanted to make it, eh? He wouldn't turn away from anyone. Some of the other guys, they didn't want to make it as bad as Shonnie. Me, I was young. I couldn't defend myself in English when they said something to me, so I just turned red, eh? I didn't go looking for fights, but I didn't back down. I *couldn't* back down if I wanted to stay."

Sooner or later every hockey player learns the game's cruel side—some well before Junior. Fred Shero, coach of the Philadelphia Flyers, reports, "I saw a *Midget* game in Toronto last year and I left after the first fifteen minutes. It was brutal. Both referees should have been put in jail. Both coaches should have been put in jail. Every time one kid touched another with the body, the other kid immediately swung at the other's head with his stick. And no penalties. Somebody was liable to get killed."

Montreal's Jim Roberts, who played Junior A hockey for the Peterborough Petes of the Ontario Hockey Association, recalls, "There were times, when I was eighteen years old, that I was really scared. Other clubs, like the Toronto Marlboros, they'd have some animals out there who acted like they were training to become wrestlers instead of hockey players. There were nights, lots of nights, when I was really scared to go out there against those guys. But somehow I got through it. And now the NHL is a piece of cake compared to those games. It's

Fighting and fouling become a way of life for a hockey player long before he gets to the big leagues. "The NHL is a piece of cake compared to those Junior games," says Montreal's Jim Roberts.

not half as rough as it was in some of the amateur leagues."

Within weeks, Paiement was back in Earlton. Harassed if not intimidated on the ice, lonely, and homesick, he might have persevered—but he got in a brawl.

"I kicked somebody in the head with my skate," Paiement recalls. "It was during a fight, eh? I didn't hurt him, but they gave me a six-game suspension anyway. So I quit and went home."

At home Paiement joined a juvenile team near Earlton, and scored 35 goals in 11 games. He stayed with his family through Christmas (always a grand celebration in the Paiement household), but by New Year's he was restless.

"One night he told me to take him to the airport the next morning," recalls Paiement, Sr. "I said, 'Where are you going, back to Niagara Falls? You gonna play there again?' He said yes. I said, 'You gonna stay there this time or are you gonna come back home?' He said no, he would stay."

The next morning Wilfred and Rosila Paiement were up before their youngest child. She prepared a breakfast of juice, ham and eggs, and milk. When he came down for breakfast, he had packed his belongings for Niagara Falls. Little was said over the breakfast table. Then the

Paiements drove their son to the airport. They were early for the plane, and while they waited they began to talk.

"Why I come home is that damn big [Eric] Vail [now with the Atlanta Flames and rookie of the year in 1974–75]," Wilf said. "He makes me mad."

"Why?" his father asked.

"He's always telling me Rosaire [then with the Vancouver Canucks] is no good. He says Rosie's beating up everybody, but when he gets up there he will kick the shit out of him."

"You're crazy," said the father. "Tell Vail to go to hell, and if he bothers you, *fight* with him. You're just as good as him, better probably."

"Oh, he's big," said the son. "He's eighteen, and I'm fifteen."

Wilf Paiement, Jr., got on the plane and went back to Niagara Falls. It was not a good year for him. When he returned, he was far behind the rest of the players in the league. However, this time he stuck it out. A few months later, Wilfred and Rosila Paiement went to Niagara Falls to see their son.

"You know what?" the father recalls. "When we got there we could not believe it. Wilf is living with big Vail. They are in the same house together. He told us that the very first workout they had when he got back to Niagara Falls, he fought with Vail. I had told him it did not matter how big Vail was. It was like me with those Gaspé guys. I was not looking for trouble, but I had to go. I was right at the end of the gun there. So I always tell my kids, do not go looking for trouble—but do not back up from it either. So we got back to Niagara Falls, and Wilf is rooming with big Vail."

Sitting in his Kansas City apartment with his father, Wilf Paiement remembered his conflict with Vail, and laughed. "He is right. Oh, Vail made me mad, saying those things about Rosie. So we fought. And we became friends."

The confrontation with Vail proved to be a watershed in young Paiement's career. The next year he was in St. Catharines, secure in the life of a promising Junior hockey player, scoring goals, and enjoying himself thoroughly. "I always like to score goals. I get a special feeling when I score a goal. In St. Catharines I lived with a real nice family—Birdie and Chris Hubbard, very nice people. I am getting forty dollars a week and room and

board. I am riding buses and having fun playing hockey."
A year and a half later, Wilf Paiement was in the National
Hockey League.

February 21, 1975, was a bright, cold, windy day in
Kansas City. The night before, Paiement had scored the
nineteenth goal of his rookie year in a 6–3 loss to Montreal at the new Crosby Kemper Memorial Arena. Only
after building a 6–0 lead in the first half of the game had
the Canadiens relaxed sufficiently for the Scouts to avoid
humiliation. Paiement's goal, with only 21 seconds left to
play, came on a rebound of a shot by Guy Charron.

The mild comeback was a source of satisfaction to
Kansas City management. With a potpourri of fuzzy-
cheeked kids, castoffs, and fringe players, the club is
aiming for nothing more than respectability, and against
one of the NHL's most powerful teams the Scouts had
made a game of it. "To the people who thought about
coming tonight and didn't," observed general manager
Sid Abel, "six to three looks a lot better in the morning
paper than six to nothing."

The Scouts would prefer to build a franchise on a
foundation of solid draft choices, but like any losing
team, they long for a little glamour to attract customers.
In Wilf Paiement, they do not have a performer with the
electric qualities of a Bobby Orr, a Gil Perreault, a Guy
Lafleur, or a Marcel Dionne. He is not a player who will
jerk fans from their seats with end-to-end rushes, or
catch their eye with the furious forechecking and play-
making ability of a Bobby Clarke. Paiement's style rests
in economy of movement, strength, and a big shot—in
giving the puck to a centerman to have it returned when
he bursts free on the wing, or bulls his way in front of
the net for a shot or a rebound.

Off the ice, Paiement is a good-looking youngster in
his way. A shock of brown hair is forever falling into
clear blue eyes, deeply set beneath dark, heavy brows.
His cheekbones are high and prominent, his jaw square
and strong. His shoulders are wide, the biceps those of
a lumberjack. Paiement's wrists and forearms are large
and powerful, like his father's. (They have much to do
with his shot, which can drive a goaltender off his
skates.) Despite his good looks, Paiement is something
of a loner. He speaks English fluently now, but he is not
one to draw crowds of reporters with quotable quotes or
the swinging life-style of a young professional athlete

with a lot of money to spend. Through mid-February of 1975, Paiement had spent only $2,500 in cash since training camp opened five months earlier. His modest apartment in the Sunny Hills development in North Kansas City has a stereo, a television set, and a grandfather clock, which he bought on sale.

On local television, and in the feature sections of the newspapers, Paiement comes across as what he is— a teenager who has been thrust into the spotlight by the big money he is making, and his potential. "Sometimes," concedes coach Bep Guidolin, "we can't get across to Wilf what we're trying to do—make him a star."

The morning after the Montreal game, the Scouts worked out for an hour at the Kemper Arena. Afterward, Paiement showered, pulled on a pair of brown corduroys, a light-blue button-down shirt, and a brown leather jacket. Then he departed for North Kansas City to see a doctor about an asthma condition that had been bothering him for a week. "It runs in the family," he explained.

In the parking lot, Paiement climbed into a bronze 1972 Monte Carlo that had not been washed for weeks. The backseat and floor were littered with newspapers and hockey equipment; the rubber mats on the front floor were caked with dried mud. The rookie pulled out of the lot, made a few quick turns, sped up the ramp to Interstate 35 north, then gunned the Monte Carlo up to seventy miles an hour.

"I could be driving a Mercedes, eh?" he said, lounging in the driver's seat with the bottom of his huge right wrist resting atop the steering wheel. "I hear [Pittsburgh rookie Pierre] Larouche has gone through five cars already. But my father, he gave me this car when I went to Niagara Falls to play Junior hockey. I like it fine. My father made a lot of money. He could drive a Cadillac if he wanted to, but he still drives his pickup truck. If I let the money give me the big head, the other players would not put up with me, and neither would my family. I was at Bobby Orr's hockey camp last summer. From being with him, you would never think he was the number-one player in the game. He does not think he is too big for everyone else. If I did, I would be nothing. People who do think that way are nothing."

The rookie acknowledged the pressure he felt as one of whom much is expected in his first year in the National Hockey League. "I never asked for this, eh?" he said. "I was playing hockey for fun with kids my age

140

when Larry took me to play in his league. I really did not want to go. Then I go to Niagara Falls, and hockey, it is not really that much fun there either. I got suspended, and quit. When I went back everybody was so far ahead of me I could not catch up. The next two years, when I am playing in St. Catharines, hockey is a lot of fun for me.

"Now it is only one year later and hockey, it is all business now. It is not fun anymore. We are supposed to win games, but you know we are not going to win that many games with our team. But I get the big money, eh, and I feel like I should be winning games for us. They are paying me to score goals, so I get real moody, real down on myself, when I am not scoring goals. Sometimes I have to tell myself that I am only nineteen years old and I have a lot to learn.

"When it is five-two, and we are ahead, I can not wait to get out there and try for more. When you are winning, hockey is a lot of fun. But when you are so far behind all the time, it is tough to keep on going. You got to work extra hard to get yourself up for the games, eh? That goal last night helped. I wish we could have won. But even though we lost, that goal helped me. I am in a better mood today because I got a goal."

Paiement admitted that at first he was thrilled to compete against the Orrs and Espositos. After a few months, however, the thrill began to fade. So did the sense of privilege from riding on chartered jets instead of buses, from staying in the finest hotels instead of boarding houses. It is not much fun to go into Boston Garden or the Spectrum, only to be blown off the ice by the superstars. As defeat piled upon defeat, and the Scouts found themselves hopelessly mired in last place in the NHL's Conn Smythe Division, Paiement began to feel like so much cannon fodder for most of the other teams in the NHL. He found himself looking forward to the end of the season, when he could go back home to the north.

The rookie laughed. "My grandmother, when I am drafted by Kansas City, she thinks it is in Texas, eh? For myself, I was not sure where Kansas City was either. When I am in Junior hockey and thinking about playing in the National league, I am thinking of Buffalo, or Toronto, or Montreal. In Buffalo or Toronto I am not so far away from home. My parents, they can come to the games, and so can my friends."

In Kansas City, and on the road trips as well, Paie-

ment began reminiscing about how he used to get up before the sun and go hunting with Larry and Ambrose; of how he used to be able to jump into the pickup truck and drive down to the lake and go fishing. In less than an hour, he would return with a string of trout that he would quickly clean and cook over an open fire. The temptation is again there, as it was in Niagara Falls, to run home.

Today, Earlton, Ontario, has a population of about fifteen hundred. There are five streets, and they have numbers instead of names. There is the body shop, run by Rollie Parent, and the creamery, operated by Olidore Fortier. Aurel St. Jean manages the liquor store, which is owned by the Canadian government. There is the La-Salle Hotel, and its tavern, where the farmers and construction workers gather after work and on Saturday night. There is Robert's Motel, two banks—the Caisse Populaire, and the Bank of Nova Scotia—an IGA store, and the post office. Katie Kerr, who runs the post office, is one of the few people of English origin in the Earlton area.

The thrill of reaching the NHL has faded for Wilf Paiement, who gets discouraged by the failures of his team. The pressures of being talented and well paid sometimes seem greater than the rewards.

"We have no theater, eh, and the restaurant closes up at ten o'clock every night," says Wilf. "But still, there is so much for me to do there, and I know everybody there. It is home for me."

When he was growing up in the north country, Wilf Paiement fully expected to go to work for his father someday, make about $15,000 a year, get married, and raise a large family. Unlike other boys his age, he was not faced with the very real threat of spending the rest of his life in the mines of the north country.

Bob Plager recalls, "My dad and my relatives all worked in the mines. I did as a kid, and it was so dark down there that all I could think was, 'Please God, get me out of here. Let me see what the world is all about.' Hockey was my only way out. So I took it."

"I come too late for all the work, eh?" Paiement says. "When I am born, most of the hard work, it is over. But my father and my mother work hard all their lives. They have earned everything that they have and they are proud of it. I am not afraid of work. Construction is good, honest work. You are outdoors all the time. I like being outdoors. I like construction—the big loaders, the big machines. I like being in charge of a job. Sometimes, when I am away from home for so long, I wonder if hockey is really worth it, eh? I don't mean just the NHL. I felt that way when I was playing Junior, too."

Though he may have regrets about it, Wilf Paiement has chosen the job of scoring goals in the NHL instead of dynamiting rocks and building roads in the north country. By most standards, his rookie year in the NHL was reasonably successful. He scored 26 goals, including 3 that proved to be winners in Kansas City's 14 victories, and another that earned a tie. If he appears somewhat disillusioned about playing in the NHL, and unimpressed with the material things he can earn by such a career, it is likely that he is really just disconsolate over playing for a loser. For Wilf Paiement, the money doesn't compensate for spending seven months of the year away from home losing hockey games.

As for violence, Paiement's experiences and feelings about the matter are fairly traditional. The NHL greeted him, as it does all its newcomers, with numerous attempts at intimidation. With ample opportunity to respond to the challenges, Paiement led the Scouts with 101 minutes in penalties. Yet, the rude indoctrination doesn't seem to have fazed him. "Hey listen," he says. "This is a rough sport—not a kid's sport. You've got to be rugged in this game. No matter how much talent you have, you have got to be tough.

"But it really has not been as tough as I expected. Maybe it is just because I am a Paiement. Everybody in the NHL remembers how Rosie could fight, and right now he's one of the best fighters in the WHA. Rosie did not go looking for fights, but he kind of liked it when he found them. I'm not really that good a fighter. I think I'm just strong. But anybody who gives me an elbow in the mouth will get it back."

If Paiement had any complaints about fighting in the NHL, it was that the other clubs seemed to be waiting until he was near the end of a shift before they challenged him, by which time he was weary from two minutes of end-to-end skating. As a result, Paiement did more grappling than punching, which was evident in a bout with Yvon Labre of the Washington Capitals, two days before the Montreal game.

"Fighting tires you out quick when you're on skates," the rookie said. "And it's even worse when you're tired to start with. Like with Labre, all I could do was tie him up and pull his sweater off."

"Yeah," said Sid Abel, "but he pulled the kid's shoulder pads off too, and almost his pants. Believe me, that's quite a trick—even when you're not tired."

At first glance, it may seem as if Paiement and other hockey players accept the violence of their game as laconically as they do the harsh Canadian winters. But it goes deeper than that. Like other shared hazards of life, violence can bind hockey players together, even as it pits them against one another on the ice. They respect the other players for their courage, and, paradoxically, they can express an almost gentle affection for the men they have grappled with.

In a sense, the elder Wilf Paiement's epic battle and subsequent reconciliation with the Gaspé Peninsula men is played out every year in the NHL. "Rosie fought Bobby Orr once," Wilf, Sr., recollects. "In the first period he cut him and gave him a black eye—seven stitches. In the third period Bobby Orr jumped Rosie again. Rosie hit him in the same spot, opened up that cut again, and seven more stitches. Oh, what a black eye Bobby had! But Bobby is a helluva nice guy. We were out to visit him last summer . . ."

5.
The Bad Guys

In his home rink he is a war hero, showered with cheers and lavished with affection. His loyalty is unquestioned; his tactics, however crude, are staunchly defended; he is never the source of aggression, only the deterrent to it. He may not have won all his battles, but in the hearts and minds of his fans he is undefeated, because he has never succumbed to fear, the ultimate failure. His scars and stitches are decorations for valor.

On the road he is a war criminal, despised because he is dreaded. He has respect for no man, no law, no property—a mercenary whose battlefield is a hockey rink. His weapons and methods are all disreputable—a stick, an elbow, a glove in the face, a sucker punch. Never turn your back on him—he can't resist an unfair advantage. He is a bully for whom the only just fate is to be bullied himself.

The bad guy himself knows he is neither a hero nor a villain. He is a tradesman dealing in agitation and intimidation in order to help himself and his team. He knows it is dirty and dangerous work. "Sure I play dirty," admits Steve ("Demolition Durby") Durbano, "but it doesn't bother me. A lot of guys do dirty things to me, too."

Glen Sather, a veteran agitator who now works for the Montreal Canadiens, remembers, "When I was with Boston and the Rangers, I always had the feeling that Noel Picard of the Blues hated me because I called him 'Mary Christmas.' [Picard was born on Christmas Day, hence the name 'Noel.'] Pic confirmed it when I got traded to St. Louis. But I figure that's part of my job— getting the other guy so mad that he forgets about the business at hand. But you'd better be ready when he decides to shut your mouth for you."

A bad guy tries to unnerve his opponent with taunts and tirades, to lull him into complacency with flattery, and to promote the spectacle with various antics. But underneath he is like a prizefighter; he understands that, inevitably, the issue will be resolved with fists, and that he may leave the confrontation bleeding, even unconscious. He knows that in his job, more than in other jobs, talk is cheap. Courage wins respect, and winning respect is his goal.

Traditionally, it is the younger players who feel the need to gain with violent fouling the respect they think may otherwise elude them. For them, the fighting game— complete with name-calling, boasts, challenges, and the

Blues' Bob Gassoff TKOs Leafs' Brian Glennie. To the young bad guy, fighting is a means of showing courage; winning the fight is nice, but secondary.

Dave Williams quickly established a reputation
as a hothead by attacking everybody,
including some mean veterans, such as Blues'
Barclay Plager, that rookies usually avoid.

inevitable denouement—is a hallowed rite of manhood.

During the 1974–75 season, Dave ("Tiger") Williams of Toronto, and Bob Gassoff of St. Louis, performed that rite in a home-and-home series between the Leafs and the Blues. Their confrontation began in a game in St. Louis, when the two players traded punches after a scuffle behind the Blues' net. Williams claimed that after he had fallen backward on the ice, Gassoff had leaped on top of him.

Referring to the game the two teams would be playing three nights later in Toronto, Williams warned, "You can tell Gassoff that he'd better be watching for me every time I'm on the ice Saturday night. I'm going to get him. No one Japs me and gets away with it. But that's the only way he'll fight you—when your back is turned and you're down on the ice. He's a cement-head, but I'll get him Saturday night. I never had a chance to get a punch in, and the linesmen kept me from fighting back. I'll get the first one in Saturday night. I promise you that."

Gassoff replied, "If he wants to fight Saturday night, I'll fight him. But he's always been afraid to fight me in the past. We played against each other for four years in Junior hockey [in the Western Canada Hockey League] and he never wanted anything to do with me. He just likes to put on a big show."

Williams is twenty years old, 5 feet 11 inches, and 180 pounds. An amateur boxer, he had acquired 310 minutes in penalties the year before, as a left wing for the Swift Current Broncos of the WCHL. Gassoff, also 20, is 5 feet 10 inches, and 185 pounds. In his last year in the WCHL, as a defenseman for the Medicine Hat Tigers, he had set a new league record with 388 minutes in penalties.

A promoter could not have arranged a better matchup: two players of like age, size, and strength, who wanted to fight. As the two teams took the ice before a capacity crowd in Toronto, the usually undemonstrative Maple Leaf Gardens fans cheerfully anticipated a battle. One sign read, "Tiger Will Turn the Blues' Gas Off."

Unfortunately for the fight fans, Toronto coach Red Kelly kept Williams on the bench for almost the whole game. During the last minute of play, with no sign of the Tiger and the teams settling for a 3–3 tie, several hundred disappointed fans started to leave the arena. They missed the highlight of the evening. With only two seconds remaining, a faceoff was called to the right of the St. Louis net. Gassoff was waiting for play to resume, his stick braced horizontally on his thighs. Later he would say that he never saw Tiger Williams come over the boards for the first time in the game.

"I was just standing there, waiting for the faceoff," he said. "Then I glanced sideways and saw some gloves on the ice. The next thing I knew somebody had belted me in the jaw."

As he had promised, Williams threw the first punch. Afterward, however, Gassoff assumed command, ripping lefts and rights to the face of his adversary. Williams grabbed Gassoff's hair in an attempt to slow the barrage, but Gassoff jerked free. At the end of the fight, which the linesmen permitted to continue for two full minutes, blood was streaming from a cut over Williams' left eye and from his lower lip. Twenty stitches were required to repair the damage.

Gassoff told the press that it was "a good fight, a clean fight," though he said he did not appreciate the sucker punch and the hair pulling. He paid no tributes to Williams' fistic prowess, but made no derogatory remarks. The fight, he said, spoke for itself.

Williams reacted similarly. There were no glowing references to Gassoff, but no alibis. He had been soundly defeated and he seemed reconciled to it. "It was a good fight," he said. 'The referees let us settle it our way."

Men, young and old, challenge each other every day. But in the case of Gassoff and Williams, the talk ceased and the two fought. Gassoff undoubtedly found satisfaction in victory, Williams some embarrassment in defeat. But the outcome of the fight was only part, and not the most important part, of the ritual. What mattered most was that the two had kept their word to one another. They had challenged one another and stood up to the challenge, proving to their teammates, to opponents, bosses, thousands of spectators, and most importantly to themselves, that each deserved respect as a hockey player because he demanded it as a man.

As newcomers to the NHL, Williams and Gassoff were two hotheaded, insecure youngsters, who embraced the fight game to prove themselves. But they were only bad guys in training. The consummate bad guy is no rookie, and he doesn't have to fight to gain respect—he already has it—and he fights only when

Gordie Howe, the master bad guy, usually got what he wanted without fighting. *Opposite top:* He decks Bruins' Bob Leiter. *Opposite bottom:* Earl Ingarfield serves as landing pad.

the privileges it accords him are challenged. The true measure of a bad guy's respect (and hence his effectiveness) lies not in how often he fights, but how much fouling he can do without fighting. In this sense, the patron saint of bad guys is Gordie Howe.

Howe never expressed his meanness in penalty minutes—getting away with fouls was part of his genius. In 25 years in the NHL he never received more than 109 penalty minutes in a season. A man of great patience, he often chose not to retaliate when abused. Instead, he mentally recorded each transgression and waited until the referee was looking elsewhere before taking his revenge. "Do you realize how hard it is to back off when somebody gives you the butt end of his stick in the corner or a two-hander across the back of your legs?" asks Minnesota's Dennis Hextall. "You get told over and over, as you develop as a hockey player, not to strike back right away, but it's one thing to be told something and another to do it. Still, you have to learn to cool it. If you get a cheap shot, hold back and take a number. Your chance will come."

Of course, Howe didn't always wait to be provoked. Once, after a game against the Red Wings, New York's mild-mannered Don Marshall was asked what it was like to play against Gordie Howe. Marshall casually lifted his shirt, pointed to a six-inch welt across his ribs, and explained, "Second period."

Eventually, Howe's reputation for discreet violence reached the point at which he was allowed unprecedented leeway wherever he skated. "The only way to stop him is to crowd him, throw him off stride," remarked the Maple Leafs' Kent Douglas. "The thing is, nobody even wants to get near the guy."

"In Gordie Howe's last ten years in the NHL no one even challenged him," says Fred Shero. "It was as if he had built a vacuum around himself. He'd get the puck and do whatever he wanted with it because everyone was afraid to get near him. It was as if they felt that challenging him wasn't worth the punishment."

Hextall says, "The idea is to put the fear of God in the boys so that they don't give it back to you, and you end up just giving it out. Then you've got the game licked. Howe was like that."

Hextall recalls an incident that demonstrated both the old man's meanness and his craftiness. A rookie with the Rangers at the time, Hextall faced off against

Howe's linemate, Alex Delvecchio, and won the draw with deceptive ease. As the rookie turned to skate behind his net, an elbow suddenly crunched him on the side of the head. "I thought it was Delvecchio who did it," Hextall says. "Nobody was going to do that to me, so I came right back with my stick. The trouble was I drilled it right into the middle of number nine.

"Three shifts later, I was going into the corner for the puck and I heard this *swoosh, swoosh* coming up behind me. It sounded like a runaway train or something. As it turned out, I got out of there just in time. It was Howe, and if he'd hit me the way he blasted into those boards, my career would have been over right then and there.

"But you know, after playing in the NHL awhile, I think those two guys just set me up in that faceoff circle. Delvecchio let me take that draw just so Howe could nail me in the head—you know, kind of welcome me into the league."

Between Howe, the master bad guy, and Gassoff and Williams, the apprentices, lies a whole range of players who play the fouling game. Some are skilled bruisers who feel they have no choice but to become hatchet men if they are to last in the big leagues. Others embrace the violent game to enhance their already ample talents. The range of bad guys encompasses men with a variety of playing styles and temperaments—from Bobby Clarke, the rink rat who fights only when cornered, to his teammate, Dave Schultz, an apparent barbarian who seems to fight for the fun of it.

"He has eyes like a cat," observed Bobby Hull of his nemesis, Bryan Watson, one of the smaller but more tenacious of hockey's hatchet men.

Glenn Sather has performed his harassment tactics
for various clubs—*above*, for St. Louis against
Rangers; *opposite*, for Rangers against St. Louis.

Montreal's Glen Sather (5 feet 11 inches, 175 pounds) and Detroit's Bryan Watson (5 feet 10 inches, 170 pounds), are relatively small rogues. They intimidate few players, but have the knack of unnerving them with an impertinent word or gesture, an annoying slash or cross-check. When they fight, it is usually against a bigger and stronger man, but the mismatch is in one sense an advantage—little men are usually beaten, and when they manage to avoid a thrashing it seems like a victory. A former little bad guy, Detroit's Ted Lindsay (5 feet 8 inches) says, "I always felt that a bigger guy had a lot more to lose than I did, because if I got lucky and floored him he was really embarrassed. His ego was really down and he was really hurt."

The small bad guy also compensates for his size with cleverness. After he has been penalized, he is particularly skillful at enticing another player, frequently a star, to join him in the penalty box.

"There are a lot of guys around the league who think I'm a little wingy," admits Sather. "They look at me as if they think I have some bolts missing. Well, that's the plan. When I'm out there they really aren't sure about what I'm going to do next, and that can prove unsettling at times."

Watson led the Central Professional Hockey League in penalty minutes with 293 in 1967–68, and topped the NHL with 212 minutes in 1971–72. He first made his mark in the majors in the mid-sixties by bringing out the worst in Chicago's gentlemanly Bobby Hull. Watson clung to Hull as closely as a sweat-soaked jersey (and a good deal more uncomfortably) and was constantly dragging the Black Hawks' superstar to the penalty box with him. "He's got a look in his eye like a cat," remarked Hull, who called Watson "Superpest." "He grabs, and he holds, and he trips. None of the other guys assigned to check me pull that stuff. He irritates me. He really does."

"I've got a lot of respect for Bobby," countered Watson, no doubt flattered by the tacit admission of his effectiveness. "He's a great competitor and a helluva guy. But when I'm given a job to do, I do it. Everyone has to make this league in his own way. Some do it by scoring goals, others by playing great defense, others by stirring things up. I compensate for the lack of great ability and size by stirring things up."

Compared to the Sathers and the Watsons, forwards

Terry O'Reilly typifies the big, aggressive forward—unafraid of getting hit, unlikely to go down without taking his attacker with him.

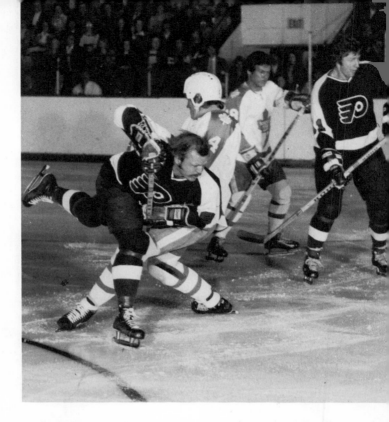

such as Boston's Terry O'Reilly and Philadelphia's Bob Kelly are bigger and stronger—and better. Their game is one of unrelenting pressure in the attacking zone and dogged backchecking, both of which they pursue with such vigor that fights frequently erupt. These players specialize in instantly invigorating a team that has become sluggish. They burst over the boards as if their energy can no longer be contained on the bench, and before long they have banished any thoughts of fatigue or laziness from the minds of their teammates. In the 1975 Stanley Cup finals, Kelly's aggressiveness earned him three goals, including the winner in the deciding sixth game.

Bigger and stronger than the Sathers and Watsons, more skilled and often more experienced than the O'Reillys and the Kellys, are the subtle foulers. They are forever thrusting their sticks between an opponent's legs, whacking at his ankles, elbowing him in the ribs, and taking special delight in getting away with it. "I think I'd call it 'cute dirty,'" says Dennis Hextall, a prime practitioner of the style. "It's the art of not getting caught. So many penalties are called for retaliation because the

Opposite: Accompanied by fellow shock trooper Don
Saleski, right, Bob Kelly arrives in the pits
despite the best efforts of Dave Dunn. *Above:* Bobby
Clarke usually lets others fight for him, but
Bert Marshall prefers to settle differences directly.

160

referee didn't see what started all the monkey business. I used to get suckered in that way all the time. Now, I'd like to think I'm capable of suckering the other guy. I've reformed a bit; reforming means I don't get caught as much.

"Bobby Clarke is that way too. I've already told him he's the dirtiest SOB in hockey today, but I don't hold that against him. That's his style and it happens to be my style as well. We both agree that when you dish it out you've got to be ready to take it. And when two players agree on that, there's really no problem."

Traditionally, the epitome of the bad guy has been the tough defenseman. Ted Green, the master backliner of intimidation, liked to say, "You build a reputation for yourself, and after a while, when a forward goes into the corner and he knows you're right on his tail, he may

Opposite: "Cute dirty" Dennis Hextall wrestles Barclay Plager. *Above:* Pat Quinn has mellowed with age but still presents an awesome profile.

swerve at the last second to avoid getting blasted. Maybe you have no intention of nailing him, but he doesn't know that, does he?"

When the stick of Wayne Maki felled Green in 1968, there were no tears shed around the NHL. "The way I saw it, he had it coming," says Atlanta's Pat Quinn, a brawny and far from innocent defenseman himself. "He used his stick like a machete, and it caught up with him. Now, if it had been somebody like Dave Keon or Murray Oliver, it would have really bothered me. Guys like that don't have it coming. You never want to see someone like that get hurt."

Although Quinn himself has mellowed somewhat with age (he is now 33), he still ranks among the bad guy defensemen. "I never could skate that well," he admits, "and I knew the only way I was going to make it in the NHL was to take advantage of my size. You do what you have to do to stay. In Toronto, Punch Imlach was a master of showing me that the other team is just trying to take money out of my pocket, trying to make me a loser. And they'll laugh behind your back if you let them do it. So when you get the chance, you smack people around. You know who the chickens are in the league, and whenever you run into them, you never let them forget it."

Among the most colorful of today's bad guy defensemen are the St. Louis Plager brothers, Barclay and Bob. "They still call our father 'Squirrel' because they think he raised three nuts," says Bob. (The other would be Billy, now in the Minnesota North Stars' chain.) The Plagers' style is not only intense (former Blues coach Scotty Bowman remarked that Barclay Plager "even schemed to win our intrasquad scrimmages") but also flamboyant. When a goal is scored against St. Louis, Barclay Plager storms about in tight circles, swearing loudly, his head twitching with rage. When penalized, he rushes to the penalty box, slams the door shut, thumps down on the bench, and buries his head in his gloves.

These outbursts are particularly delightful to the Pittsburgh fans, who serenade Plager, whenever misfortune strikes him, with the teasingly sweet singsong, "B-a-a-a-r-r-cl-e-e-e . . . B-a-a-a-r-cl-e-e-e."

"I'm the best thing that ever happened to Pittsburgh," Barclay contends. "Whenever I'm in town they pack the place."

Pittsburgh fans delight in casting Barclay Plager as

Keith Magnuson takes it on the chin from Steve Vickers. Magnuson loses many fights, but his undamped enthusiasm for provoking them is enough to make him effective.

the villain. But, as is typical of the bad guys, he doesn't really fit the part. Once, before a practice in Pittsburgh's Civic Arena, Plager shuffled out on the ice in his street shoes and joined a pickup game of nine-year-olds, prompting Red Kelly, then the Pittsburgh coach, to observe, "The fans in Pittsburgh wouldn't believe it if they could see him playing around like this. They all think he'd beat up on little kids and little old ladies if he had the chance."

Equally controversial on the ice is Keith Magnuson, who fuels his kamikaze style with aggressive thoughts well before he steps on the ice. "The day of a game, I pick out a player on the other team to hate," he says. "I think all day long about how much I hate him. It really gets me fired up. He's usually not the one I wind up in a fight with, though. He's just a symbol."

Magnuson provokes countless fights, many of which he loses, but his fighting record concerns his coach, Billy Reay, far less than his penalty record. Perhaps because he realizes Magnuson is one of the few muscle-men on his team, Reay sometimes becomes impatient when his enforcer spends excessive time in the penalty box. "I hate to see him get the misconducts, because misconducts are stupid," Reay says. "But at the same time, I can't complain about most of the fights Keith has. When a player is goading others into fights, it's generally because he's playing effectively and causing trouble for the other team. What coach could ever be unhappy with a player like that?"

Finally, among bad guys, there is a type that doesn't really deserve the name but earns it anyway—the player who fights so well that fans come to see him battle, even though opponents would rather stay out of his way. The Detroit Red Wings' Dan Maloney, probably the best fighter in the league today, is also one of the game's cleaner players. Like others who are handy with their fists, Maloney disclaims the publicity he receives from fighting, but he is one of the few whose actions support his words. "I go out there to play the game," Maloney says. "Sometimes people come out to see the players fight, but I'd just as soon have them come out to see a hockey game. You'll go into an arena for a game and someone will ask you, 'Who are you going to beat up tonight?' In that sense, fighting in hockey might be a bad trend."

Nevertheless, Maloney makes it clear that he is not

Dan Maloney's right hand is a blur as it starts
toward Don Saleski. Maloney is commonly
acknowledged to be the league's best fighter, and
for that reason, perhaps, fights infrequently.

ready to abandon the fighting game. When an opponent needs straightening out, he sees it as his responsibility to do just that. "To a certain extent, if someone on the other team is running around scaring everybody, he's the key to their chances. If he's playing good hockey, you should just try to outplay him. But if he's disturbing your team, I think someone should go out there and settle him down."

Whatever his style on the ice, the bad guy remains a working man trying to do a job that demands fearlessness and total dedication. Meting out and sustaining punishment are part of his job; so are the penalties, fines, and suspensions he is likely to incur. Yet, off the ice, like many men who work hard, he is more likely to be retiring than aggressive. Usually, he is one of the more modest, soft-spoken members of his team. Out of uniform, Gordie Howe is a warm and humorous man. John Ferguson is articulate and perceptive. Bespectacled Dennis Hextall projects the earnest air of a college professor. Red-haired Keith Magnuson is as unassuming as Huckleberry Finn.

Dave Schultz is the league's busiest fighter but not one to spear or swing his stick. *Right:* Bouncing off Blues' Richard Wilson. *Opposite:* Dancing with D'Amico.

Dave Schultz, modern hockey's premier bad guy, is in many ways typical of the breed. He grew up in Waldheim, Lucky Lake, and Rosetown, Saskatchewan. His father, an auto mechanic, went where the work was.

"Waldheim was a very religious town—Mennonite brethren," Schultz recalls. "They didn't drink, dance, or smoke. There was no beer joint there, no dances. When I was little, I went to Bible camp in the summer for about three years.

"I wasn't a tough kid. One time, when I was about eight years old, my brother and I put on boxing gloves. He hit me in the face and I quit. I remember having one fight in school. One kid was really bugging me. I took a swing at him, a slap really, because I was used to slapping with my brother. But this kid hit me with his fist. He just punched me, and I cried."

A placid young man, Schultz changed his disposition as a hockey player when he joined the Junior team in Sorel, Quebec. "That's where it started," he says. "We had a real rough Junior team. I wasn't scared. I knew everybody would back me up. The next year, at Roanoke, Virginia, in the Eastern League, I got into a fight in the first game. The other players liked it, the fans liked it, the coach liked it. I did the same thing at Quebec and Richmond of the American Hockey League, because I realized the only way I'd make the NHL was by playing tough and fighting."

Schultz made it in 1972, after having been drafted by the Flyers (fifty-second overall), in the 1969 amateur draft. In each of his first three years, he led the league in penalty minutes, and in 1973–74, he established an NHL record with 348 minutes in penalties. "The mantle fell to Schultz as the leader of the pack," Flyers general manager Keith Allen observes matter-of-factly.

Describing his style, Schultz says, "I can feel myself changing out there. It doesn't happen in the locker room, or when I skate onto the ice, but the moment someone touches me or checks me. Then something just clicks in my head. The blood starts flowing faster inside me and I seem to get twice as strong as normal."

Schultz is a classic example of the hockey player who is best known for fouling and fighting. "If the Flyers had to depend upon Schwartz for goals, they'd never win a game," fumed Chicago coach Billy Reay, after Schultz scored a goal to beat his Black Hawks.

"Schwartz?" a writer asked, incredulously.

"Yeah, Schwartz," snapped Reay. "Number eight. The left winger. You know who I mean."

And yet, though he is condemned around the league as a hatchet man, Schultz is also respected. "He's not a goon," says Minnesota's Murray Oliver, who despite his size (5 feet 9 inches, 170 pounds) has lasted 17 years in the NHL. "There's kind of a purpose to his aggressiveness. You always know when he's around, but I'm not afraid to turn my back on him in a corner. He doesn't use the stick. He's the first one to drop his stick, and there are a lot of players you can't say that about.

"I'll never forget one game against the Flyers. I went into the corner with Schultz and, in trying for the puck, my elbow caught him smack in the eye. He pulled back and I could see it had really hurt. I thought, oh-oh, here it comes. Then he said, 'Goddamm it, Muzz, just keep those f——g elbows down from now on, will you?' With that he took off after the puck again.

"Really, it was kind of funny, eh? Me, five-nine, elbowing a guy as big as Schultz. But like I said, he's not a goon. When he goes after somebody, it's usually somebody his own size. I respect him for that.

"I guess I've survived for seventeen years because I always had a pretty good idea of who I could trust out there and who I couldn't. A guy like Schultz, who's playing good, aggressive hockey, I really don't worry about him. I believe I can trust him. If he happens to hurt you, it's more likely a mistake.

"It's the goons that you've got to look out for—the guys with that faraway, kind of screwy look in their eyes. I always know who's on the ice with me. That's part of my job. But when one of the goons is out there, I know where he is at all times."

Typical of the hockey bad guy, Schultz leaves belligerence and controversy on the ice. His wife, Cathy, says her husband is "a pussycat" around the house. "He's a real Libra," she says. "They don't like emotional hassles. They don't like the confrontation situation." His hobby is assembling miniature ships in bottles.

Schultz himself admits to being embarrassed when the public ranks him, along with goaltender Bernie Parent, captain Bobby Clarke, and Rick MacLeish, as a premier member of the Flyers. "It's funny to me," Schultz says. "I never thought I'd make the NHL until I got here. Now I guess I'm as well known as guys who score twice as many goals. When you hear people talk about the

Flyers, it's Bernie, Clarke, Rickie, and me. I don't deserve to be even mentioned with them—at least not hockeywise."

Clarke says that the Flyers' notoriety "bothers some of our players, and the one it bothers most is Schultz. He can't stand in a hotel lobby without somebody walking up and calling him an animal. He's getting it ten times as much as anyone . . . and I know it hits him hardest."

Of course, some tough guys find it profitable to perpetuate their hero-villain images off the ice. When Derek Sanderson was a Bruin, he won fame and fortune by telling hockey fans what they wanted to hear from a bad guy. On the Johnny Carson Show and in other television appearances, he coolly quipped about his money, his girl friends, and his bravery. The more outrageous the statement, the more he seemed to enjoy it. Recently, Sanderson has turned scornful of the fighting game, but his comments remain as aggressively tactless as ever. It is, after all, good PR.

Chatting with columnist Hugh Delano of the New York *Post,* Sanderson made these observations: "Hey, most of the fighting is an ego trip in front of the fans. You want to fight? Okay, I'll meet you in an alley after the game. Bring a f——g gun along and we'll get it done.

"You live by the sword, you'll die by the sword. You want to be Billy the Kid? Okay—he killed fourteen guys, but he died.

"I'm more intelligent than I was five years ago, when I thought fighting was what was happening. Who needs it? Any moron can go out on the ice and beat up on guys."

Most bad guys do not favor such oratorical overkill. After doing their jobs on the ice, they usually find no use for posturing off it. And they are by no means all morons. They can be thoughtful and perceptive about their work and themselves.

"On the ice I can become an animal if I get mad," observes Buffalo's Jim Schoenfeld. "But as soon as the game is over, I forget about any of the fights I've had. Off the ice I like to meet the guys I fight with and see if they are human, like I am. When you leave the rink, you should be just a man, not a hard-hitting hockey player.

"You have to be able to get away from your business and relax. When I cross that Peace Bridge from Buffalo to Fort Erie, Ontario, on the way home, I can

Derek Sanderson, rushing to aid Brad Park, is no stranger to the fight game and the hype game. Still as loquacious as ever, he is less combative as a Ranger than he was as a Bruin.

172

feel a load being lifted off my shoulders. I unwind and I begin to enjoy the things around me.

"Truthfully, I'd like to have people come into the dressing room and say, 'You played a good game,' instead of 'What a great fight you were in.' I'm really not out to hurt anybody in a fight. I just figure it's the other guy's job or mine and I'm going to be as tough as I have to be. I might bruise somebody, but then I take my share of bruises too. That's hockey."

Says Schultz, "I have fears of my own. At times during a game, I'm scared of fighting a certain guy. Or I think that maybe this guy could beat me, and I've got a reputation to protect. But once you're in a fight, you forget all that. Things happen too fast.

"I don't really want to hurt anybody in a fight either. Oh, I like to beat them up and leave them with some

The old and the new. *Opposite:* Jean Beliveau dumps Ted Lindsay—one of the few times Maurice Richard (9) could afford to turn his back on Lindsay, whose feud with the Canadiens never waned. *Right:* Jim Schoenfeld leaves his battles on the ice.

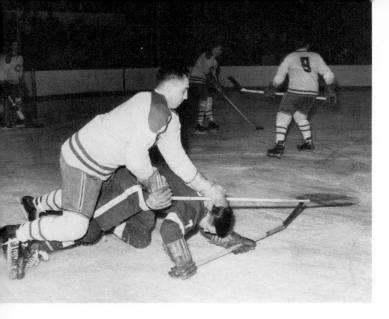

bruises and bumps, but I don't want to hurt them. One night I cut Bryan Hextall during a fight in Atlanta, and when I saw the blood, I told him I hadn't intended to cut him. I meant it. Same thing in the playoff against the Rangers in 1974. When I beat up Dale Rolfe in the seventh game, I felt bad about what I did and I told him so. He's a class guy."

Schultz may be more self-serving than accurate in portraying himself as a man of compassion, but simply in recognizing the other man's feelings he represents a significant change among bad guys. Hockey players have not always apologized for winning their fights. In fact, just a few years ago, the bad guys made hating the opposition a year-round occupation.

"Hockey is a mean, aggressive game," laments John Ferguson, who used to squirm with discomfort when forced to sit next to an opponent at a banquet. "You've got to be mean, and you can't turn it off and on like a faucet. I mean, how can you tee it up with a guy on the golf course in the summer and seriously try to knock his head off in the winter? No way—it can't be done."

Recalling his famous feud with Maurice ("Rocket") Richard, Ted Lindsay seems regretful that it's no longer as heated as it once was. "I probably continued to hate the Rocket until about three or four years ago. . . . As much as I hate to admit it, through our socializing I guess the Rocket and I have kind of melted the barrier, so to speak. I mean, we had a *tremendous* hate for each other."

Like Lindsay, Richard was a hot-blooded, cold-eyed competitor for whom winning justified almost any tactic. When Richard was a right wing for Montreal and Lindsay a left wing for Detroit, the two skated side by side for years, high sticking, slashing, cross-checking, spearing, butt-ending, and fighting one another. Together, they epitomized the heated rivalry between Montreal and Detroit, and at times it appeared as if one were trying to destroy the other before he was himself destroyed.

"For me," says Richard, "the worst player I've ever skated against was Ted Lindsay. It wasn't so much that he was a dirty player; it was that he had such a dirty mouth. He was always saying something dirty to you out there."

Lindsay confirms the charge. "I used to go to the Rocket and I'd say, 'You dumb f——n' Frenchman, I'm going to take your head off your shoulders with this stick!' And before you know it, he's forgetting the puck. He's looking for me, but at the same time I got to be looking for him because he's liable to take my head off my shoulders."

"I used to hate our home-and-home series with the Canadiens," Lindsay continues, "because after the Saturday night game in Montreal, I had to ride on the same train with them to Detroit. I can remember walking into the dining car on Sunday mornings and checking to see if somebody like the Rocket or Butch Bouchard was in there. If they were, I wouldn't go in until they had left. It was the same with other teams. Everybody would try to finish their breakfast before the guys on the other club woke up. That way they wouldn't have to bump into them in the dining car."

Such feuds were largely the products of a six-team league in which players considered themselves loyal soldiers for the organization that had sponsored them since their youth. In many cases, old-timers moved up to the NHL wearing the discarded uniforms of the parent club. It wasn't long before they developed a ferocious loyalty to the "crest."

Today, sponsored clubs have been abolished, and a player is apt to feel more loyalty to himself and to his fellow players (regardless of their team) than to his organization. Players of different clubs not only socialize in the off-season, but go into business together as partners in hockey schools. The bad guys' reputation for feuding is largely a relic of a bygone era.

Better educated, more assertive and independent, wiser and more thoughtful than his predecessor, today's bad guy has even been known to question the wisdom of his owners and coaches if they expect him to be nothing but a hatchet man.

Bob ("Battleship") Kelly of the Pittsburgh Penguins, a splendid fighter in the Western Hockey League, established his reputation in the NHL with a clear-cut decision over Philadelphia's Dave Schultz during an exhibition game in the fall of 1973. At the time, Kelly was with St. Louis, a team badly in need of his muscle.

In November, 1973, the St. Louis *Post-Dispatch* carried a small feature on Kelly, in which he was quoted as saying that he was being told to start fights with cer-

Bob ("Battleship") Kelly was stereotyped as a goon and has had difficulty shedding the image. He is one of a growing band of players who resent being used as hatchet men.

tain opponents. Kelly noted one incident in particular when, he said, coach Jean-Guy Talbot told him to "get" Toronto's Eddie Shack. "And all it got me was a call from Clarence Campbell and a fine," Kelly told Gary Mueller, the writer. "I can play the game of hockey as well as anybody on the Blues' team, but I thought if all I'm going to be is a goon I might as well hang up my skates."

When the story appeared, both Kelly and Talbot denied it. "They used to tell me to do that when I was in the minors," Kelly said. "They haven't done that since I've been in St. Louis. I'm here as a hockey player, not a heavyweight champion."

Midway through the season, however, Kelly was traded to Pittsburgh, with Ab Demarco and Steve Durbano. Kelly had scored only nine goals and eight assists in 37 games, but it was not his lack of scoring that dissatisfied management. With only 45 minutes in penalties, he was said not to have been playing tough enough to satisfy the St. Louis brass.

Kelly was not happy with the trade. He had just settled his family in St. Louis and was particularly upset at having to pull his young daughter out of school. Not long after he arrived in Pittsburgh, he again talked to the *Post-Dispatch* writer. This time he returned to his first story. "The Blues are trying to turn [St. Louis rookie defenseman John] Wensinck into a goon, just like they tried to do with me," Kelly said. "I told them if they wanted a fighter to go hire a boxer. They just wanted to use me for a dummy. They told me to 'go get this guy, go get that guy.'"

Mueller then asked Kelly why he had denied the original story on the subject. "What was I supposed to say?" Kelly responded. "When you printed the story, I was under orders to deny it. So I did. I wasn't about to risk a five hundred dollar fine or whatever they would have done to me."

Talbot confirmed that he had told Kelly to play rough, but he said that did not necessarily mean he wanted him to get into fights. "We were looking for some muscle and we expected it from him. Why do you think Pittsburgh wanted him? It doesn't mean we wanted him to fight, to be a goon, as he called it."

Durbano interpreted Talbot's explanation as a subtle evasion. "Kelly made his reputation when he beat up Schultz in that exhibition game," he said. "Now there

just aren't too many players who want a piece of Battleship. If he was going to play tough, as Talbot wanted
him to, he would almost have had to go out *looking* for
trouble, because everybody was staying away from him.''

As it turned out, Kelly is a reputed bad guy who has
become an effective hockey player with the Penguins. In
the 1974–75 season, he played regularly on a line with
Pierre Larouche and Chuck Arnason. He scored 27
goals and 24 assists, and accumulated a relatively modest total of 120 penalty minutes. ''I like it here in Pittsburgh,'' he said. ''They're giving me a chance to play
some hockey. When I came here, they told me they
didn't care if I threw another punch all year.''

So long as violent fouling remains an acceptable
means of intimidation, the bad guy will be in demand.
Clubs will want him in their lineup to provoke opponents,
to protect teammates, and, most degrading of all to
him, to hype a sagging gate. Often exploited by his
bosses and misunderstood by the fans, he will nonethe-
less continue to be respected by his teammates and
more or less accepted by his opponents.

For the bad guy is maturing. He has shown that it
is possible to be tough, rugged, and uncompromising
without constantly hating his opponents and allowing his
will to win to rage out of control. The lifelong friendship
between Islanders' Gerry Hart and the Flyers' Bobby
Clarke failed to diminish the intensity and effectiveness
with which they played against one another in the semifinal playoffs, the highlight of the 1974–75 season. On
the contrary, both played some of the best hockey of
their lives. As both said, their friendship simply had to
be tabled until the summer.

Even Ted Lindsay, one of the staunchest advocates
of the old style, seemed to relent a bit the night he was
sitting in the Montreal Forum before the 1975 NHL All-
Star Game. Ten years after quitting, he finally seemed
ready to forgive his opponents. Gazing at the end of the
ice where the Canadiens traditionally warm up, Lindsay
sighed, ''You know, I hated those guys so much I could
taste it. They thought they were the best and we on the
Red Wings wanted to prove we were better. I didn't
think of it then, but as I look back to those games we
had in the Forum, I realized that those goddamm Canadiens only wanted what we wanted—to win and be the
best.''

Conclusion:
Violence
without Chaos

Thison book began with the observation that hockey
has always been a violent game. For good and
ill, violence is a hockey tradition. Violent body
contact can make a fast game disciplined; violent fouling can transform a disciplined game into chaos. The
challenge facing the game today is not to remove the
violence, but to control it so that the inevitable hard
knocks don't escalate into the incidents that ruin the
game and threaten the players. It can be done.

To its credit, the National Hockey League has taken
two positive steps to curb excessive violence on the ice.
The first was the "third man rule," by which the first
player to intervene in an altercation between two others
receives an automatic game misconduct penalty. This
rule has all but eliminated the bench-clearing brawls
that once marred hockey, and it has reduced the effectiveness of the game's so-called bad guys. It has also
made some traditional instigators less anxious to provoke
fights, knowing that if they cannot finish what they start,
a teammate won't be coming to their rescue.

The second rule, instituted before the 1974–75 season, forces a penalized player to go directly to the
penalty box without arguing or stalling, or be liable for
an additional two-minute minor. This rule has minimized
the chances of an argument erupting into a fight.

Throughout the 1974–75 season, the NHL also made
strong efforts to penalize the instigator of a fight more
severely than a player who, when challenged, merely
tried to defend himself. "When two men collide, drop
their sticks and gloves, and go at each other, it's automatic five-minute majors for both," says NHL Referee-
in-Chief Scotty Morrison. "It's when one wants to go
and the other doesn't that we're trying to establish a
differential in their penalties. They both may get five-
minute majors for fighting, but the instigator will get an
additional two minutes. Or maybe the instigator will get
five and the player who was only trying to defend himself
two.

"In about thirty percent of the cases involving major
penalties in 1974–75 we were successful in differentiat-
ing between the penalties. At the beginning of the year,
we were thinking in terms of forty or fifty percent, but
since no statistics had been kept on this sort of thing
in the past, perhaps our ambitions were somewhat
unreasonable."

These measures indicate that the NHL is not committed to mayhem. But the league has only just begun to eliminate excessive fouling. The evidence is conclusive that as referees try to limit the fouling while preserving the action, fouls not only go undetected, but are frequently overlooked, tolerated, and even tacitly encouraged. The result is a game that is suffering because its excesses are at best haphazardly regulated by a referee who is frequently not in a position to control them.

It is not the referee's fault—it is the fault of the refereeing system. Professional hockey needs another referee. Basketball has two officials, baseball four, football six. Yet in "the world's fastest team sport"—which is, indeed, so fast that it is impossible for one man to see, let alone call, every foul—only one man calls penalties. Hockey could accommodate another official, whether by adding another referee and dispensing with one linesman or simply by empowering linesmen to call any penalty.

Perhaps hockey would find it profitable to use basketball's system of one referee following the play and the other leading it. Whatever the most practical two-referee system, it would limit each man's responsibility and increase his efficiency. Because each referee would have a better position from which to make the calls in his area of responsibility, more fouls would be caught and more nonfouls let go. In particular, referees would be in a better position to catch the instigators and thereby eliminate the notion among the players that they must retaliate when abused.

As a team, two referees would be less susceptible to home-crowd pressures, first because they would have more confidence in their ability to be in position, and second because each would gain some moral support from his partner. In baseball, football, and basketball, referees are grouped in teams that work, travel, and in some cases live together for as long as a whole season. In hockey, what *esprit de corps* referees might share with linesmen is dissipated because the combinations of officials change each night. The linesmen and referees are isolated not only from the players and fans, but also from one another. Says Bruce Hood, "When you're alone so much, you tend to think too much. You start worrying about things you shouldn't. For me, the loneliness and the waiting are the toughest things about being a referee in the National Hockey League."

The President of the National Hockey League, Clarence S. Campbell (a former referee himself), recognizes the problem. "Who does a referee go out with if his linesmen have to leave after the game?" Campbell asks. "Well, he'll probably go out by himself. And sometimes that can be like going out with his own worst enemy. He made mistakes during the game. Of course he did. He's a human being. But, unable to talk to someone about those mistakes, he might start playing them over in his mind, building them out of proportion—second-guessing himself, wishing he'd done something else. That's when a referee can be heading for trouble; it could affect his next game and the game after that.

"After a particularly rough night, a referee just doesn't go back to his hotel and fall asleep. He collapses from physical and emotional exhaustion."

In the long run, such torture may make the man a better referee, but it is an inefficient as well as a brutal means of improvement, especially in view of the fact that, with far less trauma, other sports produce equally competent officials who control their games better.

Why does hockey persist in the one-referee system when the cost to the game and to the referees themselves is so great? The answer seems to lie in tradition—the tradition of rugged individualism that hockey has always cherished. Says Campbell, "These are very special men. They're like the old Spitfire pilots—hard-fisted, strong-willed—bringing the plane in on the seat of their pants. They're instinctively capable of handling tight situations. A referee in the National Hockey League must have iron in his soul."

Compare this image to that of football referees, those short, almost dowdy fellows who look a little ridiculous as they scurry among the behemoths. Individually, they project an air of anything but heroism, yet as a team, they are highly motivated, efficient, and above all respected.

Hockey has much in common with football. Both have a tradition of violence, even brutality. Football refereeing has advanced with the sport, adding officials as increases in speed, changes in strategy, and common sense warranted. As a result, football officials now firmly control their game without dominating it. Hockey too has evolved. Today it is faster and more complex than ever before. Yet the league contents itself with glorifying the referee while undercutting him.

Of course, there are objections, besides those based on tradition, to adding another referee. NHL executives appear to distrust a team concept of refereeing. They admit that there are now dramatic disparities in the way different referees call games, but they claim that pairing referees would only make matters worse. "What worries me with regard to two referees on the ice at the same time," says Scotty Morrison, "is that they may very well differ in philosophy. Say you had a Ron Wicks, who is fairly strict in his interpretation of the rules, and someone like [former referee] John Ashley, who used to pretty well let them go. You would have two different philosophies at different ends of the rink, and this could lead to real trouble. It might even come down to a particular call in which the players are asking, 'Who's right?' You might even have one ref upstaging the other now and then, calling penalties that the other didn't call, simply because he saw it from a different angle."

Dividing responsibilities among teamed officials could pose a problem, but other sports long ago overcame it.

In basketball, the referee under the basket watches for violations close to the hoop, while the referee near midcourt catches most of the fouls on the perimeter. If one official happens to see a foul or violation in another man's primary area, he is free to call it. In football, the responsibilities are broken down even further. The referee, who is in overall charge of the game, cannot make the decision for another official on a judgment call unless that official asks for help. In both football and basketball, the lubricant that makes the system run smoothly is teamwork. Working in concert, with a thorough understanding of each other gained through months, even years of partnership, the officials know each other as well as a quarterback knows his favorite receiver. It takes hard work and practice, as well as compatible personalities, to form an efficient team, but the result is not only greater efficiency from each team, but a greater degree of standardization among all of them.

Each team has its individual characteristics, but the supervisors of officials in football and basketball don't find different "philosophies" of foul calling among their officials. When a rushing defensive lineman in football decks the quarterback, it is either roughing the passer or it isn't, and whether Tom Bell, Norm Schachter, or Pat Haggerty is making the call should make no difference. There is a standard to be adhered to, so what is a foul to one ref should be a foul to another. Only in hockey is there a wide range of interpretation of fouls. In pro basketball, the officiating has drawn criticism for lack of consistency, but significantly, no one has advocated going back to the one-referee system. Indeed, the National Basketball Association has experimented with a three-referee system.

Other sports have proved that a well-coordinated team of officials is far more effective than any one man, but hockey executives insist that it wouldn't work in their sport. They point to the brutal first Team Canada-Russia series, when two referees were used in each of the games, but failed to catch some of the most blatant fouling. Some observers even felt that each referee undercut the other by making calls to appease one side when it felt that the other referee had been unfair.

This is a convenient but weak argument against two referees in NHL and WHA hockey. From an officiating standpoint, the Team Canada-Russia series was a debacle, but it was no fair test of the two-referee system. In each of the games, one official was chosen from a Western country and one from a Communist-bloc nation. Despite a crash course under Morrison and his assistant, Frank Udvari, they were unfamiliar with one another's style. And their experience in international play proved wholly insufficient when they were confronted with the mayhem of a grudge match between the best players in the world. If nothing else, they simply couldn't keep up with the furious pace. Ian MacLaine reported in the *Canadian Press,* "Morrison thought that even under the North American system of one referee and two linesmen that the skaters were moving at such a fast pace that the officials would be hard-pressed to keep control."

The whole sorry experience proved that poorly prepared referees—under any system—cannot mediate a political squabble. It did not prove that two referees won't work in the NHL. To say that a two-referee system could not be adapted for pro hockey is simply not to give it a chance. To pretend that one highly skilled but inevitably flawed human being can do the superhuman job of officiating a pro hockey game is to ignore the game's most serious problem. The league may take more steps to reduce excessive violence, but until it overhauls its refereeing system, allowing officials to call the fouls more efficiently and consistently, it is only likely to add to the problems of men who are already some of the most overburdened officials in all of sport.

Instituting a better officiating system is the first step. The next is to enforce the distinction between fouls the NHL acknowledges to be "aggressive" and those that are truly defensive. As the rules are enforced today, a player caught high sticking or slashing is subjected to a two-minute penalty, no more than the player found guilty of holding or tripping in center ice. By Rule 58 (C) of the NHL rule book, referees are instructed to award a five-minute major for high sticking that results in "injury to the face or head of an opposing player," but majors are rarely assessed unless blood is drawn.

In recent years, the NHL has recognized the inflammatory nature of butt-ending and spearing by making them *automatic* major penalties. The same could be done for high sticking, cross-checking, and slashing—the other fouls that entail the abusive, often dangerous, use of hockey sticks. Or, if these fouls were deemed less dangerous than butt-ending and spearing, they could be penalized by *automatic* double minors. The key is to take discretion away from the referee in penalizing these fouls while encouraging the officials to call them whenever they occur. Obviously, the referees will tend to be reluctant at first because such a severe penalty may affect the game even more dramatically than their other calls. But if all the teams are sharply forewarned, the referees should have no more trouble calling majors or double minors for high sticking, slashing, and cross-checking than they do now for spearing and butt-ending.

If the league were cracking down on slashing and other abuses of the stick, Darryl Sittler might have realized that slashing Lafleur wasn't worth four or five minutes in the penalty box. If Darcy Rota had known that an elbow to the jaw of an injured player would draw a penalty (perhaps a match penalty if the referee saw it as a deliberate attempt to injure), he might have kept his elbow out of Oddleifson's face.

Interestingly, one man who supports penalties of greater severity for abuses of the stick is Fred Shero, one of the architects of a style that exploits the weaknesses in the game's officiating system. Says Shero, "I think if a player cross-checks you with his stick, it should be a major penalty instead of a two-minute minor. That would help. Get rid of the high sticking and cross-checking, get rid of that, and our game is all right."

Scotty Bowman, coach of the Montreal Canadiens, says, "The hockey stick is for shooting, passing, and receiving the puck, not for swinging. The puck is on the ice, not up around somebody's head."

With the crackdown on abuses with the stick, other aggressive fouls such as elbowing, roughing, and charging need not increase if the teams understand that referees will be vigilant in calling them.

Pro hockey could drastically reduce fouls of violence without changing the game's rough-and-tumble nature. The answer is not to try to take the violence out of a game that is inherently violent, but to control the violence more efficiently and judiciously, by (in order of importance):

1.) *Instituting a system of two referees in order to catch every foul and interpret borderline cases more consistently, without regard to which team is the home team, which team is winning, or the balance between the teams of penalties already called.*

2.) *Penalizing the dangerous and provocative fouls of cross-checking, slashing, and high sticking more severely—with either automatic double minors or majors—while strictly policing other fouls intended to intimidate (roughing, charging, elbowing, etc.).*

3.) *Continuing to penalize the instigator of a confrontation more heavily than the retaliator.*

With the adoption of these measures, referees could control a hockey game without feeling they were ruining it. The effect would not be to take the hitting out of hockey, but merely to change it from cheap shots to clean, though violent, checks. Players and coaches know the difference. They need only be encouraged to observe it.

"A player doesn't mind a good body check," Shero says, "that's part of the game. But the high sticking when the referee doesn't see it, or overlooks it, that's what really gets annoying to a player. It gets so annoying that he just can't take it anymore. And if he does keep taking it, he's going to get run right out of the league."

Fighting or stick swinging is the player's response to fouls the referee missed, not to legitimate body contact. An offensive lineman in football gets bashed on every play. Although he is protected more heavily and moves more slowly than a hockey player, the punishment he takes from body contact is roughly comparable to that of a hockey player being body checked. Yet only rarely does pro football erupt in fighting. There are fouls, even missed fouls, but in general, football players have the confidence in the referees and rules structure to control the fouls. There is good reason to believe that with similar confidence in hockey's refereeing and rules structure, hockey players would also accept hitting without feeling the need to fight.

Says Shero, "Hitting is part of the game—legal hitting. If you don't hit legally, you get a penalty. So that's the law, those are the rules, *and players want to play by those rules* (emphasis added)."

Even in the touchy area of checking goaltenders, hitting can be preserved without provoking fights if rules-makers and referees make it clear that goalies really are fair game once they stray from their crease and should be expected to check and fend for themselves. Or the goaltender's customary privileges can be safeguarded by incorporating them in the rule book, and enforcing them on the ice. In either case, fouling and fighting don't have to be a form of justice supplemental to officiating.

Many hockey people believe that because stick swinging is more dangerous than fighting, it alone should be more strictly regulated. Few players have been seriously wounded from fights in which sticks were not involved. Indeed, NHL executives go so far as to say that without fighting as a safety valve, players would be more abusive with their sticks, and thus the game would become more, rather than less, violent.

In the swirl of controversy over what to do about fighting, the question of what causes it is often neglected. It is said that players fight because they are frustrated, or because they are rewarded for it, or because they are trained to, or because they can get away with it, or because they are glory hounds. All of these explanations have some truth, but they make the most sense as part of a more powerful reason. Many players start fights for the same reason they swing sticks: because they are afraid *not* to—afraid of being thought a coward, afraid that only by the stick swinging or fighting can they gain or keep respect and stay in the game. If hockey removed their fear, it would eliminate much of the stick swinging *and* fighting. Without the incentive to do one, players are not likely to do either.

However, most players have come to accept fighting

as part of the game, and no matter how efficient and strict the refereeing, hockey players are not likely to abandon fisticuffs overnight. For this reason if for no other, a ban on fighting would do more harm than good. It might, as hockey executives persuasively suggest, lead to more stick swinging and other fouling. And, of course, there would be an outcry from some fans and a sense of keen disappointment in many more who enjoy the scrapping.

Fighting has been a part of hockey since the game's inception, and there is no good way to make it instantly disappear. The way to deal with fighting is not to try to suppress it all at once, but to undermine it gradually. There need be no self-righteous proclamations about stamping out the evil of violence, just a quiet commitment to upgrading the game by rewarding players for hard-hitting but clean hockey. The fighting would decrease, and hockey, far from losing its appeal, would find that it doesn't have to market brawls to sell itself. Pro football has shown that a violent sport can not only attract fans without fighting, but sell itself as a game of master strategy as well. Hockey could do the same. By encouraging the players to play by the rules, the league would be promoting not a less popular brand of hockey, just better hockey. And as anyone who has watched a good hockey game knows, that is the best sell of all.

A Rebuttal by Clarence Campbell

NATIONAL HOCKEY LEAGUE

920 SUN LIFE BUILDING · MONTREAL, P.Q., H3B 2W2 · (514) 871-9220 · TWX 610-421-3260

PRESIDENT'S OFFICE

Mr. Jeremy Friedlander
Rutledge Books
25 West 43 Street
New York, N.Y. 10036

July 23, 1975.

Re: "The Violent Game"
by Gary Ronberg

Dear Mr. Friedlander:

As you are aware from our telephone conversation, I received your letter of July 8th (received on July 14th) along with the galley proofs of Gary Ronberg's new book and you have requested me to provide you with "only my honest reaction" to it.

Because I lay no claim to competence as a literary critic, I must follow your request literally and this will result in a series of rather disjointed observations—some favourable, but mostly critical.

Frankly, my total reaction to the book is one of disappointment. I had been so impressed with Gary's previous book in which he had captured perfectly the real spirit of the Game at all levels of participation among the players, officials and spectators. He skilfully analyzed its ingredients and presented it for what it is—the greatest natural spectator sport in the world—not for the number of its devotees, though they are legion, but because of its characteristics of speed, skills, violence, colour and continuous action. Perhaps, in the circumstances, I expected too much of this latest effort—more than was reasonable.

In trying to discern what went wrong, it is my impression that Gary did not give himself nearly enough scope. "Violence" is only one facet of Hockey and certainly NOT one of its most important features, in spite of the efforts of some who have sought to make it appear so. The extent of actual physical violence which occurs in the average NHL game is quite minor compared with the sheer violence which occurs in football and yet it is hard to imagine a book devoted exclusively to violence in football. What could it be but a recital of its consequences and their intimidating influence on the way the game is played? Everyone knows that it is a violent game in which the violence itself has been refined almost to an art form. So it is in Hockey, but it hardly warrants several hundred pages of text to prove that its history is full of violent incidents—especially as the number of such incidents has steadily declined in the last quarter century.

One major contribution which Gary has made in this book, for which many will be appreciative, is that he has given to "violence" in Hockey a new and more accurate definition—one which relates to the way the game is played rather than raw and sometimes vicious aggressiveness which less discerning observers have mistakenly described as its principal characteristic, which is not the case. I am sure that this new definition will help its aficionados, both professional and amateur, to understand it better.

My assessment of the book starts with a feeling of resentment against the title—"The Violent Game"—because in my opinion it misrepresents Hockey as it is played in the NHL. Of course, it is a violent game in the same sense that football is violent. But it is not the violent game in the sense that violence is its principal characteristic or that it is the most violent game—which clearly it is not in terms of either continuous physical impact or the extent of the injuries sustained by the participants which renders them unfit for play.

Secondly, I challenge as unfounded the charge (p. 75) that "hockey has failed to regulate itself" so that "civil authorities have felt the need to step in. Other sports have taken the necessary steps to control, if not eliminate excessive violence. Hockey has not."

What evidence is submitted in support of this charge? The launching of a criminal prosecution by one District Attorney against one player in one game out of 9,000 games played in the last 30 years. As this case is still sub judice, it would be improper to discuss it. Suffice it to say that the result of that proceeding has done nothing to indicate the need for the intervention of the civil authority. When compared with Juan Marichal's assault on John Roseboro with a baseball bat or the number of players felled every year by "bean-balls," one has to wonder what makes the Forbes actions so dastardly as to require a public prosecution. The fact is that Hockey (NHL) has responded promptly and effectively to a number of types of violence that have broken out from time to time—e.g., stick swinging, spearing, bench clearing and fighting. These actions are a matter of record which have made the League's standard of discipline socially acceptable.

In my judgment the chapter devoted to the "Paiement saga" is both untypical and inappropriate. It is altogether proper to investigate and comment on the family background of hockey players to illustrate their environmental upbringing, even the violence which may have, to some degree, moulded their character. But to use Père Paiement, who, as far as we know, never participated in a hockey game in his life, and to cast him in the role of a typical paternal influence on Canadian hockey players who are bred to violence and originate from the mines and the backwoods of Canada, is simply a travesty of the facts. Such a misrepresentation is totally unwarranted.

It is difficult also not to experience some resentment at the way the author has pontificated about the shortcomings of the officiating and the bold assertion that "Hockey needs another referee." This is compounded by the cavalier way in which the opinions of the Referee-in-Chief on this subject are dismissed (p. 183). The presentation of this subject in the book would leave one with the impression that the "two referee" system is some magic formula suddenly contrived to materially reduce or eliminate fouling. Such an impression is completely out of harmony with the facts about officiating. During the first 15 years of the expanded NHL (1924–1939) the NHL used the "two referee" system and discarded it for the very reasons given by Referee-in-Chief Morrison. It produced in every such pair of officials (they usually worked in pairs) a stronger referee and a weaker referee (a leaner). Their overlapping jurisdiction, their varied reaction times and often their different philosophies about the conduct of the games led to a complete separation of their functions by the League in 1939—one Referee and one Linesman. This prevailed until after the introduction of the red line (1943) when it became necessary to add another linesman.

While Gary's text does not say so, I assume that what he is really campaigning for is four officials—two Referees and two Linesmen—which, in my opinion, will not reflect favourably on his views concerning officiating generally. Even he will have to acknowledge that it would be pretty ludicrous to have 4 officials overseeing the actions of 12 players! There is not sufficient space to accommodate another official and he is NOT necessary. There is plenty of space for extra officials in both football and baseball—but not in Hockey.

The reason why I am so adamant against what Gary calls the "two referee" system is because I worked as a Referee in that system for years as an amateur and for 4 years in the NHL (1936–1940) and I have personally experienced all of its shortcomings.

Finally, I must challenge the implication in the last paragraph of the book that the NHL has to "market brawls to sell itself." This is "the unkindest cut of all" and I do not believe that Gary really believes it either. The NHL has never tried to build up the gate with "brawls" or any other form of violence because we had a complete Standing-Room-Only position prior to "expansion" and we quickly developed that position as "expansion" progressed. The Game itself has been more than adequate for this purpose. No special stimulus has been necessary.

In the result, you will probably evaluate these observations more as a rebuttal than as an assessment of the book. If so, I can only say that these two concepts are inseparable in this context. I have taken exception to some material in the book because I think it misrepresents Hockey in fact. I imagine Gary's response will be, that that is a matter of opinion. Anyway, you now have "my honest reaction" and I can only hope that this will prove helpful and useful to your purposes.

Yours sincerely,

C. S. Campbell
President

CSC:t
cc—Mr. Gary Ronberg

Appendix

NEW YORK RANGERS, 1973–74

	W	L	T	Pts./Pctg.	Power Plays	
Home	26	7	6	58/61.7%	For	222/48.2%
Away	14	17	8	36/38.3%	Against	239/51.8%
Total	40	24	14	94/100%	Total	461/100%

First Power Play After a Score

	Rangers Score		Opponents Score	
	Rangers PP	Opponents PP	Rangers PP	Opponents PP
Total	47/37%	80/63%	58/52.7%	52/47.3%
Home	35/44.9%	43/55.1%	29/67.4%	14/32.6%
Away	12/24.5%	37/75.5%	29/43.3%	38/56.7%
Dif. btwn. Home & Away	20.4%	20.4%	24.1%	24.1%

Power Plays While One Team Was Leading

	Rangers Lead		Opponents Lead	
	Rangers PP	Opponents PP	Rangers PP	Opponents PP
Total	84/43.0%	111/56.9%	65/52%	60/48%
Home	65/51.2%	62/48.8%	24/55.8%	19/44.2%
Away	19/27.9%	49/72.1%	41/50%	41/50%
Dif. btwn. Home & Away	33.3%	33.3%	5.8%	5.8%

PHILADELPHIA FLYERS, 1974–75

	W	L	T	Pts./Pctg.	Power Plays	
Home	32	6	2	66/58.4%	For	257/35.5%
Away	19	12	9	47/41.6%	Against	466/64.5%
Total	51	18	11	113/100%	Total	723/100%

First Power Play After a Score

	Flyers Score		Opponents Score	
	Flyers PP	Opponents PP	Flyers PP	Opponents PP
Total	40/23.5%	130/76.5%	50/45.5%	60/54.5%
Home	22/23.4%	72/76.6%	28/65.1%	15/34.9%
Away	18/23.7%	58/76.3%	22/32.8%	45/67.2%
Dif. btwn. Home & Away	−.3%	−.3%	32.3%	32.3%

Power Plays While One Team Was Leading

	Flyers Lead		Opponents Lead	
	Flyers PP	Opponents PP	Flyers PP	Opponents PP
Total	108/34.4%	206/65.6%	71/42.7%	95/57.2%
Home	67/36.2%	118/63.8%	24/51.1%	23/48.9%
Away	41/31.8%	88/68.2%	47/39.5%	72/60.5%
Dif. btwn. Home & Away	4.4%	4.4%	11.6%	11.6%

(Statistics based on scoresheets provided by Rangers and Flyers.)

Acknowledgments

This book would not have been possible without the cooperation of numerous professional hockey players, coaches, executives, officials, and writers. There are those, however, who went out of their way to be of particular assistance—Sid Abel, Scotty Bowman, Clarence Campbell, Bob Casey, Bill Chadwick, Dick Dillman, Cliff Fletcher, Jack Gordon, Punch Imlach, Dave Kostrzewski, Ted Lindsay, Scotty Morrison, Gary Mueller, Chuck Newman, Murray Oliver, Pat Quinn, Jim Roberts, Fred Shero, Art Skov, and Frank Udvari.

I also wish to thank Evarts Graham, Jr., David Lipman, and Mrs. Joan Foster Dames of the St. Louis Post-Dispatch for the freedom granted me to work on this book. Jeremy Friedlander, of Rutledge Books in New York, deserves special recognition for the concept and structure of the book itself. He was generously assisted by Walt MacPeek, who supplied valuable information and equally valuable moral support, and by the competent public relations staffs of various clubs, particularly John and Janet Halligan and Art Friedman of the New York Rangers.

Finally, I want to extend a personal note of gratitude to my wife, Chris, for her patience and understanding during the months in which the book was planned, researched, and written.

Gary Ronberg

Photographic Credits

Alexandra Studios 9; **Wayne Crosslin** 80a, 80c; **Melchior DiGiacomo, Cyclops Photo** 2–3, 4–5, 27, 28, 30, 33, 38, 41, 46–47, 51, 53a, 55, 60, 70, 76–77, 79, 80b, 80d, 87, 90, 90–91, 97, 105, 107, 111, 112–13, 114, 116–17, 118, 119, 124b, 141, 144–45, 153, 154, 155, 157, 160, 161, 163, 167, 171, 172, 175, 179, 181, 183, 184, 187; **Darwin K. Garrison** 124a; **Graphic Artists** 71, 82, 134, 136, 158; **Fred Kaplan** 26, 48, 50, 56b, 83; **Bernie Moser, Dufor Photographers** 109; **Wilf Paiement, Sr.** 120–21, 126, 127, 131; **Rich Pilling** 179; **Photography Inc.** 19, 64–65, 84–85, 86–87, 165; **Paul Renshaw** 123; **United Press International** 11, 13, 14, 18, 20–21, 25, 34, 44–45, 53b, 69, 73, 94–95, 99, 100, 101, 102, 110, 147, 148, 151, 159, 166, 173; **Wide World Photos** 23, 29, 56a, 57, 72, 98.

Front and back jacket photos by Melchior Di Giacomo

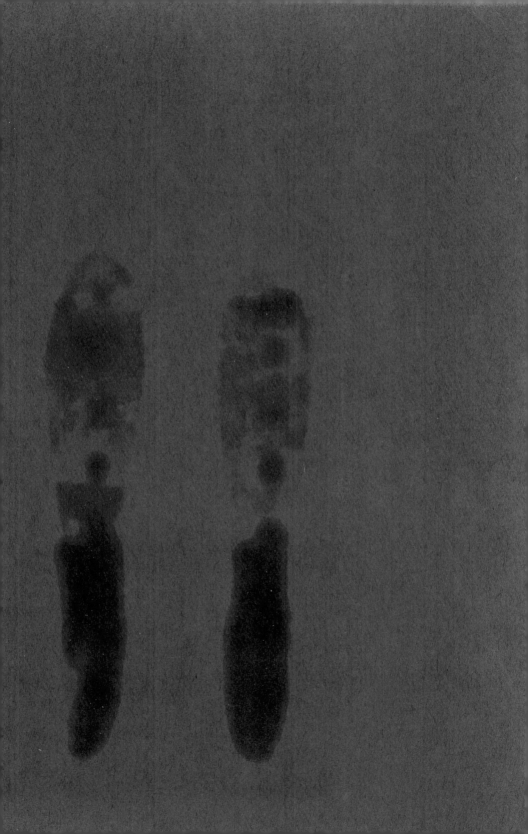

	DATE DUE		